AN AMERICAN RENAISSANCE

DISCARD

An American Renaissance

A STRATEGY FOR THE 1980s

JACK KEMP

HARPER & ROW, PUBLISHERS

NEW YORK, HAGERSTOWN
SAN FRANCISCO, LONDON

1817

Grateful acknowledgment is made for permission to reprint:

Excerpt from article by David Stockman. Reprinted with permission of the author from *The Public Interest*, No. 53, Fall 1978, pages 3–44. © 1978 by National Affairs, Inc.

   Excerpt from editorial "Tax the Rich" reprinted with permission of *The Wall Street Journal*. Copyright © 1977 by Dow Jones & Company, Inc. All rights reserved.

AN AMERICAN RENAISSANCE: A STRATEGY FOR THE 1980s. Copyright © 1979 by Jack F. Kemp. All rights reserved. Printed in the United States of America. No part of this book may be used or reproduced in any manner whatsoever without written permission except in the case of brief quotations embodied in critical articles and reviews. For information address Harper & Row, Publishers, Inc., 10 East 53rd Street, New York, N.Y. 10022. Published simultaneously in Canada by Fitzhenry & Whiteside Limited, Toronto.

FIRST EDITION

Designer: Sidney Feinberg

Library of Congress Cataloging in Publication Data

Kemp, Jack.
An American Renaissance
   1. Income tax—United States. 2. Government spending policy—United States. I. Title.
HJ4652.K38 1979   336.2'42'0973   78–19825
ISBN 0–06–012283–8

79 80 81 82 83 10 9 8 7 6 5 4 3 2 1

To my benefactors—patient instructors in the art of government, the citizens of the 38th District of New York . . . and to my most important political contributor, my wife, Joanne.

Contents

Acknowledgments

In the days before government became such an important part of our lives, a politician could spend his leisure hours with pen and paper, composing an agenda of political ideas. In the renaissance of America, I hope those days will return. Meanwhile, I gratefully acknowledge the substantial contributions I had in writing this book: Jude Wanniski, in helping to organize the effort; Alan Reynolds, John Lenczowski, Bill Schneider, and John Mueller in assisting with the many drafts; Irving Kristol, Art Laffer, Bob Mundell, Jeffrey Bell, Norman Ture, M. Stanton Evans, Paul Craig Roberts, and Representative David Stockman as primary sources of ideas and wisdom; Randal Teague, Bruce Bartlett, Spencer Reibman, and Steve Entin for technical and creative assistance; Donald Rumsfeld and Larry Silberman for their sensible reflections on the manuscript; Mike Scully, for his editing polish; Sharon Zelaska and Susan Summerall, for their patience in organizing my time to take this book from conception to birth; and my wife, Joanne, for her usual perception and wise counsel.

AN AMERICAN RENAISSANCE

1   *A Republican Revolution*

This is a book about the American renaissance, about the revival—already under way—of a strong, prosperous, proud America. And so this is a book of optimism, of hope, of national renewal. In a phrase, this is a book about the American Dream, that amalgam of promise and effort and desire that made this country the hope of civilized peoples everywhere.

Unlike most dreams, the American Dream was not mere fancy. Wherever people were invigorated with its message, good things happened. It was a dream that brought results—and still can. Not long ago, every American, almost without exception, could trace for you his or her family's history of ascent. That is to say, their personal histories of dreaming and achieving.

Here in America was the one place on earth where you could climb as far as your abilities could take you, unimpeded by your lack of noble birth or laws of entail and privilege that separated the people of other countries from their God-given right to pursue the good things in life and claim a portion of them for themselves. If you were a first-rate carpenter or mezzo soprano or football quarterback, and you gave it your best—here, if anywhere, you'd make it. And if you didn't make it to the very top, perhaps because you didn't try hard enough or the natural talent just wasn't there, at least you were better off for the attempt. A lot better off than that vast majority of mankind that never had a chance to do their best—or even to do what they wanted to do—with their own lives.

Opportunity, the chance to make it and to improve your life, that's what the American Dream was and is all about. What poisons that dream is when government stands in the way, throwing up roadblocks that are really unnecessary. More and more people sense along the way that they're not going to fulfill their potential, not because of a deficiency in their ambition or ability, but because of a deficiency in the political structure. Their honest ambitions are frustrated. They believe, often rightly, that somehow the flaws of government have held them back or cut them down.

What really gripes is that we also know it is not a case of an individual sacrifice for the good of all. That we could understand and appreciate when it is necessary. But more and more there is the feeling that the system is so fouled up that neither the individual good nor the collective good is being served. Instead of government serving to create a climate of opportunity, acting as the impartial referee dispensing justice, we now sense that government has become the competition. Our government is the other team—and it's winning!

Now, I happen to be a Republican. In fact, I happen to believe that our American renaissance requires for its fulfillment the revival of the Republican Party as a first-rate political force. But that requires that we Republicans face up to the truth of our part in shaping our current national predicament. The hardest, most important step for Republicans to take is to recognize that we can't go on blaming the Democratic Party.

There was a time when I thought Democrats and their policies were the root of our problems, but I don't any more. Rather, I realize that Democrats have been running the show *because they have been beating Republicans.* And when Democrats beat Republicans it is for the same reason that the Yankees beat the Dodgers or the Steelers beat the Cowboys: *They were better at what they did.* Why? Because for many years Republicans rejected competition as the test of value in the political marketplace. That's when the GOP got in real trouble. You still hear from some Republicans that Democrats win because the poor ignorant voters just don't know what's good for them, or that democracy won't work because the voters don't want to elect the good guys. Nonsense. Badmouthing democracy is the occupational disease of political losers.

The sad truth is that for too long Republicans beat a mental retreat from leadership. Remember, for example, the "Constructive Republican Alternative Proposals" of the mid-1960s? After Barry Goldwater went down to defeat as the Republican presidential nominee in 1964, the "moderates" and the "progressives" in the party stepped forward with a host of ideas on how to rebuild the party. I was in the middle of my first career, in professional football with the Buffalo Bills, and was not yet on the political scene. But from a distance it seemed to me that the Republicans were giving in to the idea that what the voters wanted from the Republicans was not more competition, but less.

Republicans would try to be more like Democrats, which meant more spending, more taxes, more government standing between the individual and the American Dream. Did the Democrats want to build public housing for the poor? The GOP would build public housing for the middle class. Did the Democrats want food stamps for the poor? Republicans would have to provide lunches for the middle class. Did the Democrats want to educate the poor? Republicans would have grants to blanket the middle class with low-interest government loans and tax credits for Middle America's tuition.

The Republicans could not win this competition. For one thing, the GOP's "progressive" wing could never persuade the whole party to join in. There was instead a long internal party struggle for identity. The voting public saw chronic confusion, relieved on rare occasions by moments of genuine teamwork.

At least until recently, America's domestic politics remained divided—one might almost say paralyzed—by opposing views of the Depression and the New Deal. The post-1964 rift in the GOP was in fact another demonstration of that economic calamity's lingering effects. One side could offer nothing new of its own, but counseled cloaking Democratic ideas in elephant suits; other Republicans desired the repeal of the safety net of social services first strung up by the New Deal and endorsed and re-endorsed by electorates ever since. Yet if the country can't afford Republicans who spend like Demorats, neither can it afford to have one party pledged to perpetual naysaying. While Republicans have been agonizing about public spending, unbalanced budgets, and federal deficits, Democrats have been devising new spending programs and new regulations. Remarkably, each party has fallen into a habit of neglecting what for Americans ought to be a central concern of their domestic politics: economic growth.

If one political party concentrates on increasing public spending and the other party concentrates on decreasing public spending, who is left to concentrate on economic growth, on the expansion of opportunities that can come only from such growth? Who is left to prevent the American Dream from becoming a distant memory in an increasingly segmented, selfish, Europeanized politics—the kind of which Jefferson was so fearful? This is why a Republican revolution is so important, and why it can only come as the GOP increasingly focuses its intellectual resources and political skills on generating a climate for economic growth. Republicans must commit themselves boldly and relentlessly to real economic expansion, to the growth of opportunity, and with that a return of hope.

Think about a wagon. It is a simple but forceful way of visualizing an important aspect of government. The wagon is loaded here. It's unloaded over there. The folks who are loading it are Republicans. The folks who are unloading it are Democrats. You need both groups, both parties. The Democrats are the party of redistribution. The Republicans must be the party of growth. It is useless to argue, as some libertarians do, that we do not need redistribution at all. The people, as a people, rightly insist that the whole look after the weakest of its parts. This is a primary function of collective action, of government.

The system works best when each party does its job. But instead of loading the wagon, some Republicans have jumped aside to complain about how fast an unloading job the Democrats have been doing. Other Republicans have argued that it's more fun to unload, and the trouble with the GOP is that it spends too much time complaining about the unloaders when it should be helping unload.

Obviously you can't unload a wagon faster than you load it. Sooner or later it's empty, and while you're then living from hand to mouth, the unloaders will complain. They will persuade the populace that since the loaders have failed, what you need is a new system of loading, one that rewards collective effort instead of individual effort. The next step suggests itself: Nationalize the wagons.

It is not enough that the Republican Party somehow survives. It is not enough that it enjoys a mild success, that it only wins enough elections to hang on as a minority political party. What is really necessary to the system is that the GOP become the *dominant* party in America during the 1980s. I don't mean this as a partisan, but as an American. And I mean it only in the sense that the GOP must be the party of growth, and growth must dominate redistribution in the decade ahead. The emptying wagon must soon enjoy a period of bountiful years.

When we discuss growth, *real* growth—not inflated, "paper" growth—we are talking about the American Dream. The Democrats, the unloaders, do not really understand the mechanisms that lead to real growth. (To be fair, the Republican sensitivity about social programs has been similarly unimpressive.) But because Democrats have dominated the system for generations, their idea of growth has become the conventional one. They picture an America, already gobbling a third of the earth's mineral resources, gobbling more. *Growth is seen as the exact opposite of redistribution instead of its prerequisite.* Growth must be fought and prevented, according to the new Malthusians, otherwise the planet will be stripped clean to provide the handful of humanity that resides in North America with three-car garages.

This isn't what I mean by growth. This isn't Republican growth. It's what we get when Republicans are *not* doing their job and the Democrats are trying their hand at growth. It is inflated growth, with public debt and printing-press money pumped into the wagon. It is not to be sneered at, however, when the choice is inflated growth or no growth at all. People seem to prefer inflationary growth to contraction, and contraction is what we get when Republicans climb onto the wagon to do nothing but exhort Democrats about balanced budgets. Inflated growth means *quantity* growth. Real growth, the kind that must be promoted if democratic capitalism is to survive, is *quality* growth. The difference is crucial. Quantity can only grow at the expense of the planet. Quality is a boundless concept. The same number of molecules that make up an O. J. Simpson can be an all-time National Football League halfback or "an also-ran," a successful politician or a loser. The same mineral resources can go into an automobile that breaks down after 50,000 miles and one that lasts for 150,000 miles. The difference is only in the human ingenuity that went into the fashioning of each auto.

When the American Dream is alive, this application of human ingenuity is operating near its potential. A thousand people can grow up to produce opera, Broadway musicals, or a *Wizard of Oz*. A few generations later, with government in the way, a thousand people are born to create; but of the fraction of these who survive the system, many end up making porno. Instead of several thousand restaurants worthy of three stars in the New York *Times*, we get ten thousand plastic restaurants. In so many ways, the failure of Republicanism over the last few generations has resulted in a collapse of quality and a substitution of quantity.

The golden ages of theater and Hollywood did not wane because individuals forgot how to be talented and creative. Among other causes, they were smothered by government, by postwar tax rates that punished success, and by regulations that blocked efficiency. Nor is there much on the record to indicate the Republican Party put up a fight to prevent this from happening. I think the American people would not be unhappy with another golden age of film, theater, art, and literature. Not necessarily more books written by authors with one eye on the tax codes, but books of high quality. Not bigger, more powerful TV sets, but quality programming. These are only a few of the things a prospering people can produce and afford, benefits encouraged by an economy undergoing *real* growth but stifled by economic stagnation and inflation.

Inflation shortens people's time horizons and narrows their vision. Long-term plans, say, to build a new factory, are paralyzed by the unpredictable value of money. Wealth is capriciously redistributed away from the productive investments of prudent savers and toward those who instead got deeply into debt in order to beat price increases, to hedge or speculate. By rewarding the least constructive types of economic activity, inflation lowers the economy's incentive and ability to produce more and better goods and services.

These are some of the ideas behind the tax-rate-reduction bill I sponsored in the 95th Congress with Senator Bill Roth of Delaware, and which I have revised in the current Congress. The legislation—a one-third cut in federal income tax rates over three years and reductions in business tax rates—is not intended as a measure to simply "stimulate" the economy. It is not meant as a one-shot boost of consumption so people will buy more autos or TV sets. It is rather the beginning of the process of restoring incentives in our political economy by a transfusion of fresh economic thinking. The Kemp-Roth proposal aims at removing a barrier between effort and reward, and thereby increasing the willingness of individuals to supply the marketplace. The resulting competition will boost the quality as well as quantity of goods and services.

President Carter and many Democrats have charged that such tax-rate cuts would be inflationary. But what can be inflationary about removing burdens from the folks who are loading the wagon? As Margaret Bush Wilson of the NAACP puts it, "Inflation is not caused by too many people working." Yet in terms of the "demand management" thinking—inspired by the work of the British economist John Maynard Keynes in the 1930s—that is the focus of U.S. economic policy, the basic cure for unemployment is inflation, and the basic cure for inflation is unemployment. It may seem that I must be stretching the truth, revealing a partisan prejudice. But I am not. This inflation/unemployment tradeoff is as close as the Democratic Party has come to understanding growth.

Unhappily, the idea had also infected my party, which is why Republicans have so often advocated austerity (unemployment) as the only way to combat inflation. That dismal period in the Republican Party is ending, however. The GOP is in the process of rediscovering growth, and with the rediscovery is coming a political success it will not soon forget. The cornerstone of that growth is this crucial insight: Instead of high tax rates with low production, government can raise the same amount of revenue through low tax rates applied to the high production base that will result from lessening taxes and increasing incentives. The party is beginning to be rewarded at the polls, and will continue to be rewarded, by an electorate that has been patiently waiting for us to remember that oppressive tax rates are economically destructive and politically unpopular.

This process of rediscovery was advanced by the Proposition 13 citizens' initiative in California last year, which sounded a coast-to-coast appeal for a solution to oppressive tax rates. In responding to the nationwide appeal, the Republican Party will continue to drive toward reductions in unnecessarily high tax rates: Virtually every 1978 Republican congressional candidate endorsed the Kemp-Roth bill in his or her campaign for office—a sign that a revolution is indeed taking place in the GOP. By the middle of the 1980s, I believe, the highest rate on the personal income tax will be 25 percent or less. There should be no tax at all on capital gains, and sharply reduced rates on gift and estate taxes.

Does anyone doubt that the American people would

respond to the incentives that such reasonable tax rates would provide? Does anyone doubt that there would be an explosion of *real* economic activity? The entrepreneurial talent, the managerial talent, the creative talent of men and women that is now boxed into mediocrity would be unleashed and would flourish. Real prosperity would help rebuild and renew America's cities through private initiatives; and government revenues would become available for a host of needed public projects in our cities and across our states. It would help reduce inflation. The wagon would load up with quality goods, and instead of widespread fears about the deficits of the Social Security system, there will be solvency, with funds for expansion of public and private retirement benefits. For a nation's elderly can never be secure unless that nation's young are realizing their potential in a way that provides resources across age and class lines.

Is this only a pollyannish dream? Not at all. It is a vision built not on a wish but on hardheaded logic. If we only stop what we have been doing to destroy ourselves by destroying incentives, we can once again thrive. *We are the most free and most educated, creative, talented, energetic, and healthy people on earth—and we are now operating at less than half our potential, perhaps less than a third our potential!* There's no telling what we can accomplish if only the government would get out of the way and let us load the wagon. The American Dream is not a sniveling, envious hope that everyone be leveled with everyone else. It is the freedom and encouragement to climb as high up the ladder of opportunity as possible, and obtain a just reward based upon our efforts and abilities.

What is the political mechanism underlying this Republican revolution? How does it become the dominant party? How long does it take? What will this new Republican party look like?

Instead of Republicans becoming more Democratic, I think we'll see Republicans becoming more democratic. People like democracy. Democracy, you might say, is good politics. This is so trite it's almost cute. But we Republicans have to accept the absolute fact that we have become less democratic in outlook as a natural result of losing elections. The party has resisted ideas to broaden the franchise or expand the referendum and initiative processes to the national level. But winning elections does wonders for restoring a party's faith in democracy.

When someone's approach to politics is even slightly undemocratic, as the GOP has been as a party, his outlook becomes elitist and patronizing. For years I have been hearing fellow Republicans, usually the party's theoreticians, talk about "broadening the party's base." This has a nice democratic sound to it. But the programs that flow from the idea are almost always patronizing. Blacks, for example, are assumed to be not politically astute enough to vote Republican, too eager for public handouts, so we have to lure them into the party with goodies. How about some low-interest loans for promoting black capitalism? Or let's search out young blacks and teach them how to win local elections, and maybe twenty years from now we'll have a crop of conservative Republican blacks ready to try for national offices. Or let's spend a few million dollars on television commercials selling the idea that Republicans are willing to talk to black people. And of course none of this ever works and the party's base never gets broadened, because blacks are smarter than GOP theoreticians. As far as they are concerned, the Democrats are the guys unloading the wagon and the Republicans are the guys in the wagon yelling at the Democrats. No contest.

The GOP must of course broaden its base. The only way this has a chance of working is if, to begin with, Republicans get it into their heads that people are just as shrewd in the political marketplace as they are in the economic marketplace. If you build a better mousetrap or if you offer a superior political platform, the world will beat a path to your door. You have to advertise, naturally. The party has to broadcast that it is once again offering growth. But it has to keep the quality of the product at the center of its attention, and think of political advertising not as a propaganda tool, a device for shaping minds, but as a means of broadcasting the political menu. Economic growth (real, not inflated) can't lose, and the Democrats know it. The idea is too powerful. When the NAACP endorsed growth in the fall of 1977, coming out against the Malthusian energy plan cooked up by the Carter administration, the Democrats acted as if there had been a sellout. But Republicans were just as shocked. It had not occurred to most Republicans I know that the NAACP would be in the market for growth and that the idea would sell itself.

This, I am convinced, is only the start of things. *There is a tidal wave coming equivalent to the one that hit in 1932, when an era of Republican dominance gave way to the New Deal.* It's going to happen and happen soon, and we'll find millions upon millions of Americans of every racial and cultural background surprising themselves by voting Republican. Not because they've been lured by handouts, but because they see in the GOP a better shot at the American Dream.

Is it crazy to suggest this? We forget, for example, that until 1932 the Republican Party was the home of black Americans, the party of Lincoln, of economic growth, of civil rights, of equal opportunity; the Democratic Party was still mired in Reconstruction mentality, implicit defenders of white supremacy, the Solid South and the Ku Klux Klan. Franklin D. Roosevelt did not disown Dixie Democrats in 1932, but when it came to a choice between Republicans offering marginal advances in civil rights and Democrats offering a New Deal on economic policy, a little bit of growth and a lot of redistribution, the Democrats won over black America. Older black leaders, those born in the 1920s, still remember the black Republican preachers preaching furiously against the Democrats and the New Deal, threatening hellfire and damnation for those who would desert the party of Lincoln. It was no use. Blacks were as smart then as they are now. Hoover offered a balanced budget, and FDR offered buttered bread. Just wait. It will not be long before the Democrats are forced to preach hellfire and damnation against a tidal wave of blacks voting for the GOP and growth.

In a roundabout way this brings us to international affairs, for what messed us all up in the Great Depression was the GOP's narrow nationalism, perfectly exemplified by the Hawley-Smoot Tariff Act of 1930. Herbert Hoover gave in to narrow protectionist pressures and in so doing helped engineer the economic contraction of the 1930s, for the tariff in effect closed off foreign nations' best export market—the U.S. Economic growth is not compatible with political isolation and nationalism. We can forgive Hoover on the grounds that the United States was then just beginning its role as world leader. But there would be no excusing the GOP a second time. Fortunately, the political lesson of Hawley-Smoot is still fresh enough to keep most of us from sinning, and the rediscovery of growth is so fresh and exciting a prospect that within the party it will overwhelm the pressures for protectionism.

Yet world leadership is something more than not doing wrong. If the Republican Party is to make amends for dropping the ball in the 1930s, it has to take global leadership seriously, for its mental retreat from leadership has had global ramifications. When it came to international affairs, there was a strong tradition in the GOP that said, "Not interested." This would have been fine if the Democrats were of the same mind, but they were not. The Democrats, who do not understand economic growth, have spent decades running around the world advising all the emerging nations, the underdeveloped nations, that the best way to load a wagon is to fill it full of debt. Can we blame Democrats for wanting to aid the poor and deprived of the planet? For cooking up a dozen different foreign-aid schemes, most of which did more harm than good? No. *Don't blame Democrats for advising the world on economic growth when Republicans not only had forgotten what they knew but also refused, as a matter of policy, to be of help in the domestic economics of other nations.* What has it gotten us? The Third World is now up to its ears in debt, it has not yet learned how to load a wagon, and it loathes the United States for having taught profligacy so well. The Republican Party has to take its show on the road, with a new kind of foreign aid that advises the world about economic growth and demonstrates the possibilities of the American Dream.

You see, I really do believe that it is *natural* for human beings to desire to better their condition. I sincerely believe that the American Dream is the human dream given a chance and a place to happen.

I grew up watching it happen. Before I was born, my father had sold seed to the farmers in our area of Southern California, and then after a number of years started a motorcycle sales business with my uncle. During the Depression, when, I suspect, motorcycle sales were not at their peak, my father and uncle wisely decided to branch out. They began a "same-day" service that delivered packages by motorcycle. In a few years this sideline of theirs had grown to the point that the motorcycles had to be replaced by a new mode of transportation that could carry more packages. That is about the time I was starting to take an interest in the world, and an early lesson was in—whether I knew the phrase then or not—what was meant by a "capital investment." In our family it was a new truck, and as the years passed, more and more, until we had a fleet of a half-dozen or so. As I worked with my father and brothers on weekends and after school, I grew to admire the economic system that made it possible for us to succeed by the combination of diligent effort and a good idea. And as I got older and saw that small family business my father and uncle had started twenty years before put me and my three brothers through college, you can be certain my admiration increased.

Yet my family's story, like yours, is a story of people, not of systems, no matter how extraordinary. That's why when I hope for or speak for a Republican revival I know it can never be born of "growth politics" alone, any more than I would have wanted my father to be concerned only with his business. All of us are rather a web of thoughts and desires, needs and motivations; and so a healthy political party—like a healthy family—must harmonize those complexities.

Republicans can't be a party merely of growth, nor Democrats merely of spending. Such exclusionary thinking always leads to perverse attempts to expel prodigal sons or administer ideological saliva tests. The way I think of it, each of the two parties must offer a full "catering service." Each must offer reasonable proposals to load *and* unload the wagon. In a properly functioning politics, both parties take some account of the whole range of human needs—so that the debate not only points out the differences of opinion but also the common focus of concern: people—their families, their future.

Our national debate desperately needs fresh and exciting ideas, and I think that the Republican Party is best suited to presenting them. I believe as well that if it does present them, and with the right attitude, the voters will trust us again—with both the White House and the Congress. This is what this book is about: ideas for the next decade and beyond, ideas I believe can generate a renaissance, not just for one party but for our country and its people.

2 "A Rising Tide Lifts All Boats"

President John F. Kennedy captured precisely the American viewpoint when he conceived the epigram "A rising tide lifts all boats." It inspires a feeling of betterment and, more important, of unity—a blossoming with fragrance enough for all.

But that message seemed to die with President Kennedy. Public life in the 1960s degenerated into "the politics of confrontation"—as newsmagazines of the period called it—a perversion of politics that pitted one group against another. Unfortunately, it is a style that now pervades the Carter administration, and the reason, I think, for President Carter's unsteady popularity.

In the beginning of his administration, we hoped for something more from Jimmy Carter. During his run for the Democratic nomination in 1976, he seemed to be a son of the strong Southern populist tradition. Frankly, I was moved by his speech in July 1976—when he accepted the Democratic nomination—for it was free of divisiveness. He spoke to us of a general advance, of all Americans moving together as a family. Not coincidentally, his popularity was never higher. Then, for whatever reasons—to placate the factions within his own party, or from a deeper misunderstanding of presidential responsibility—the message faded.

Senator Russell Long—a man literally heir to the Southern populist tradition—likes to say that there are only two ways to make people equal in terms of income: "You either make the rich poor, or the poor rich!" Actually, confrontation politics often claims to do both (although it winds up merely impoverishing everyone). And so the Carter tax plan gave rebates and tax credits to lower income groups *by taking them away from everyone else.* When trying to extend price regulations to natural gas that is consumed in the state in which it is produced, his Energy Department would justify their effort by promising that the action would benefit consuming states *at the expense of producing states!*

To be sure, President Carter is not alone in his misconception. Among the malarky currently adrift is that producers are pitted against consumers, and that farmers prosper only at the expense of city dwellers. Some would have us believe that the interests of most blacks are different from those of most whites—which is nonsense. Bumper stickers in the Southwest say, "Freeze a Yankee," while some Northeastern politicians kid themselves into thinking that the stagnation in their states is caused by too much economic growth and prosperity in the South and West.

All of this, to my way of thinking, represents the greatest obstacle to opportunity and advancement we face as a nation: static thinking, the idea that life is a "zero-sum" game. According to this view, there are only so many jobs to go around. Only so much energy to go around. A fixed amount of prosperity, and a fixed amount of poverty. And so it is government's job to divide up these fixed amounts until, say, the sum of prosperity (a plus) and poverty (a negative) comes to zero.

Applying this misunderstanding to sports helps demonstrate how thoroughly silly it is. The football fan knows, for example, that there aren't a fixed number of touchdowns to go around. The only limits are time and the potential of each player on both teams. The play is always pushing against the limits of time and potential, and it is the exception rather than the rule that the struggle ends much before the final gun sounds. In baseball, where time is not a limiting factor, it has become a cliché that "the game isn't over until the last man is out," meaning it's at least possible to turn failure into victory when there are two out in the ninth and you are ten runs down. Football, baseball, and other competitive sports are not zero-sum games. Neither is society.

But throughout the ages, people have been afflicted with political rulers who have treated society as if it were zero-sum. Individuals can only benefit at the expense of others. Nations can only advance at the expense of their competitors. Politics becomes the art of pitting class against class. Rich versus poor. White versus black. Capital versus labor. Sun Belt versus Northeast. Age versus youth. Gentile versus Jew. Consumer versus producer. The lesson is given throughout history: If there are no political leaders around pushing for "a rising tide that can lift all boats," there will be a zero-sum politician in the wings ready to stir factionalism and distrust.

What I'm really driving at is that there are only two ways to approach public governance: statically and dynamically. And in every nation, among every people, whatever the system of government, there are powerful tendencies toward static thinking that must be overcome by dynamic thinkers.

In Germany after World War II, only after the holocaust and the crushing of Hitler did we see this political dynamic at work in the hands of the Finance Minister Ludwig Erhard. The German economic miracle was founded on Erhard's idea that the German people should not waste their political talents and energies arguing over how to divide up the economic pie, but rather they should concentrate those talents and energies on making the pie grow. And they did.

To this day there are eminent economists prepared to argue endlessly over just what specific Erhard actions boomed postwar Germany. Was it his tax reform? Was it his monetary reform? Was it the Marshall Plan? Was it a combination? And which had greater or lesser effect? But what I'm saying is that I believe it was Erhard's rallying the people to a dynamic idea, a commitment to growth and expansion, that began the process and made it possible. *If the government of any nation is not committed to dynamic politics, growth, general expansion, and consensus rather than coalition thinking, then whatever policies it advances or attempts to advance will inevitably be halted by factional strife. This is the road we in the United States have been traveling for the past dozen years or more.* There are different gradations. Different degrees. But President Carter and Presidents Johnson, Nixon, and Ford have all been distracted from dynamic, expansionary ideas or have been consumed wholly by static zero-sum approaches to governance.

They all operated with the best of intentions, by the way. Lyndon Johnson's Great Society effort was built on an invigorating, exciting, but nonetheless erroneous, idea that government sharing can end poverty and urban squalor by taxing away resources from the "haves" and giving them to the "have nots." As is usual, the resources were taxed away from middle-class Americans and, except in the rare instance, never got to the lower-income classes. Giant federal bureaucracies were established to run programs and dispense funds that would lead to this Great Society, and by the time the federal tax dollar got through the bureaucratic "in" and "out" baskets there were left only nickels and dimes. The war on poverty became a war on the middle class—and on the poor.

Where tax dollars were actually spent, there almost always occurred an increase in bitterness and frustration in the segment of society that was supposed to benefit. All over the nation poor blacks, Hispanics, and whites, were trained by government bureaucrats for jobs that didn't exist in the private sector. Urban renewal meant that low-income housing, designated "substandard" by government bureaucrats, was torn down to make way for gleaming new—and taxable—offices, factories, and shopping malls. In 1979, a dozen years later, the nation is pockmarked with the razed acreage of defunct projects. Those evicted generally had to fend for themselves, and because they usually could only move to housing they could not afford, the federal government had to begin new programs to transfer income to citizens it had displaced. And since only a tiny number of such projects resulted in the expected taxable properties, the unlucky people whose properties surround the pockmarked urban-renewal areas now have to pay off bonds floated to ravage their towns and cities.

Every action has a reaction, and the reaction to Lyndon Johnson's Great Society was Richard Nixon's "New Federalism." I confess to being fascinated, as a freshman Congressman, with this political reaction and in a small way being part of it. But like the Great Society scheme, Nixon's New Federalism came out of a static framework.

The New Federalism's rationale went something like this: There's only so much power in government, let's take a bunch from Washington and give it to towns, cities, and states. "The federal government," folks were fond of saying back in the late 1960s, "is good at raising money, but inefficient at spending it." With hindsight, the result was sadly predictable. The administration that gave us static political thinking exhibited static economic thinking: The tax-raising budgets of 1969 and 1974 were immmediately followed by severe recessions.

When it came to economic growth—and not a few other major policy questions—each of our last four Presidents has shared a zero-sum static outlook. Do we remember President Johnson as a growth President? I don't. Do we remember President Nixon as a growth President? I don't. Or President Ford? From the time of President Kennedy's death, the Democratic Party has been fascinated with distribution, and spending has jumped stunningly. What has consumed the mostly conservative Republican political leadership throughout all the years of my political consciousness has been the overriding desire to hold back that spending—which nonetheless increased markedly even during Republican administrations.

The static zero-sum mentality that gripped my party— both its "liberal" and "conservative" wings—was not limited solely to the struggle over federal dollars. The 1970s, remember, began with the breakdown of the international monetary system. Again as a young Congressman, I was fascinated by the economic theory that President Nixon bought in 1971. The dollar, he was advised, was "overvalued" relative to the currencies of Germany, Japan, and almost everyone else. We could become more competitive, he was told, by cheapening the dollar. Instead of "exporting jobs" we could "import" them. In other words, there are only so many jobs in the world, and we want our share. This is static thinking. Today we can see how wrong it was for us to think in these terms, especially now that we've gotten poorer with this devalued and ostensibly "more competitive" dollar, and the Germans, Japanese, and Swiss have gotten richer with their "less competitive" currencies. Yet static thinking grips the Carter White House and Treasury Department, and he and his economic team still argue that there will be a silver lining, at some vague future point, in a declining dollar.

In the eighteenth century, these kinds of approaches to international economics were called "mercantilist." The crowned heads of Europe were sold on the idea that their individual countries were being held back from prosperity by the prosperity of the other countries, and that the prosperous countries were prosperous because the poor countries were buying goods from them. The "obvious" solution: The poor countries threw up tariff walls so their people couldn't buy from the prosperous countries. The result, though, was always *general impoverishment, with the poorest countries hurt the worst.* And at the end of this march to poverty waited war and revolution.

Ironically, though most individual citizens think and act "statically", I really believe they want their political leaders not to be static. The individual American knows deep down that the zero-sum game is a losing proposition for everyone, but he or she also knows that if everyone else is struggling for a piece of the ever-shrinking economic pie, he has to be in on that struggle too or wind up with nothing. It's "dog eat dog" in a contracting economy. The desire for more humane economic circumstances is why the individual citizen yearns for political leadership that can figure a way out of the paradox. Collectively, the people will support that leadership when it appears with a plan to raise the tide.

Put another way, I can't really blame my steelworker constituents in Buffalo or the management of Bethlehem Steel for pleading a case for protection against foreign steel. They're fighting for their economic lives in one competitive corner of the global market. In the same way I've got to sympathize with the pleas for import relief from shoemakers, machine tool makers, from textile manufacturers, from glass and electronic industries. In the global economic squeeze, they're getting squeezed the hardest of people here at home. And when at times one industry or the other gets some measure of import relief, I'm generally not sorry to see it happen, if only because it indicates that they were in such sad shape that the political process had to keep them from going under. But I won't support such protectionism. Indeed, I pit myself against it as hard as I can. Because without political leaders to stand up to protectionist pressures, there would be a tidal wave of protectionism, and we'd all go under as we did in the 1930s—when the Depression followed on the heels of the Hawley-Smoot Tariff Act of 1930.

The national AFL-CIO leaders, who are protectionist by tradition, find it puzzling that most factory workers around Buffalo vote for me. The only way I can explain it is that those constituents of mine know protection is not the real answer to their problems but merely a short-term zero-sum reprieve. *The answer, they tell me, is a general economic expansion, a freeing of the country's resources in a way that removes the squeeze, and thereby removes the need for protection.* In short, a rising tide. As long as I'm working for that kind of answer, I think they'll stand by me. Should I ever stop, they'll pitch me out. If I weren't advocating ideas to improve the lives of all Americans, I'd be forced to play the zero-sum game and focus solely on grabbing all the protection I could for western New York at the expense of the whole country. On issues like this, you can't be both kinds of politician.

Nobody knows better than the person in the street, the average American, who it is that finances government benevolence. We are all aware that when the government "helps" the elderly it does so by taxing the young, and when it helps the young next week, it does so by taxing the elderly. It taxes resources out of the cities to help the farms, and then taxes the farmers to help the cities. I've never met a voter in my district who has asked for assistance who wasn't perfectly aware that the assistance would have to come out of *somebody's* hide. Senator Russell Long has another favorite saying that seems appropriate here: "Don't tax you, and don't tax me. Tax that guy behind the tree."

For a conservative Congressman to survive, much less thrive, in a blue-collar, normally Democratic district, he at least has to be consistent. It has to be "Don't tax you, don't tax me. Don't even tax that guy behind the tree." After all, the guy behind the tree always finds out from Internal Revenue. Once you start apportioning tax burdens and benefits inconsistently, you are no longer permitted to play consensus politics—looking for solutions that benefit everyone. You're forced to play coalitions—not caring that your "solutions" damage the minority, just as long as you retain majority support. *Most of the political decisions made in the United States at the national level in recent decades have been the result of coalition politics.* As long as political freedoms are intact, this is certainly tolerable. But it seems awfully inefficient, for it means that every individual has to organize a dozen different ways to defend himself against all those other fellows.

To younger Americans, factionalism is so much a part of the political landscape that they imagine it was always so. In the era in which they've grown up, the fellow who does not organize to defend himself gets stuck with everyone else's bill. It seems everyone in the country is forced to join a multitude of "special interest" groups. All it means is that an unnecessarily enormous amount of America's time and energy is devoted to paying each other's bills. Literally millions of the most talented, intelligent, and educated of the nation's citizens are employed in this process. The wise guy's solution to solving the unemployment problem by having everyone take in his neighbor's washing is now part of the nation's economic fabric. Lawyers, accountants, lobbyists, political trouble-shooters, trade associations, and professional associations have always been an important part of the democratic process. As the 1970s come to a close, though, I sense that the citizenry's rebellious mood toward government has much to do with the incredible economic and psychic costs of maintaining this anti-government layer, which necessarily grows and grows with each new failure by government.

The people, after all, demand at least approximate justice, and they will fight to get it if they are shortchanged by government. It is in this light that I find it hard to get furious, as many of my colleagues do, at, say, Ralph Nader and his army of lobbyists. Or Common Cause, which turns out to be an association of associations. When the economic pie shrinks, everyone in the economy organizes more desperately for a share of what remains. Almost every other day I hear of another new association of businessmen, a new band to save capitalism from Ralph Nader. On alternate days, it appears, the Nader groups, the Sierra Clubs, the Common Causes multiply as well— to save America from the business associations. It makes the competition fierce. Taken as a whole, it tears at our social fabric. It must end. But when will it end?

The process has to end with a change in the White House: either a change in heart and attitude by its present occupant, or a change in the occupant. The United States has not had a President since John F. Kennedy who really tried to practice consensus politics instead of coalition politics, who kept an eye out for ways to raise all boats, to even things out from the bottom up. For a while, some

Americans thought Jimmy Carter would be that man, that President. Yet as I write these reflections, he seems bent on moving further and further from that idea, that ideal. We in the House and Senate must do our share to restore that ideal. But I was elected to serve my district and the people of New York, first and foremost. As long as they entrust me with their interests, I have to stand up and protect them from zero-sum politicians who think the way to help their constituents is at New York's expense.

The President, after all, is the only politician in the land who is elected by all the people. (The Vice President gets a free ride.) If he does not practice consensus politics, but tries to solve national problems by pitting groups against each other, the entire country is forced to settle into a confrontation posture. Those who act decently find themselves sacrificing more and more of their due to keep peace. Eventually there are not enough of them around to make any difference. The spirit of charity is strangled as the selfish prosper. When every day you wake up with the feeling somebody is going to try to take a piece out of your hide before the sun goes down, you stop trusting people; fellowship and charity vanish. We become a nation of loners. The national sport becomes jogging, the most efficient way to exercise in solitude, while you prepare your daily defenses against your fellow citizens and your government.

Far more important than any specific policy, I think, is the President's fundamental philosophy of government. He can have a "liberal" bent or a "conservative" bent and be enormously popular—as were Presidents Kennedy and Eisenhower—given the same people in the same country in the same time in history. But as clever as his liberal or conservative specifics might seem, he can't really be serving his country well unless he radiates, in substance and in style, the concern for all which assures that nobody gets left behind. This is what consensus politics is all about. On the surface it may seem as if it will take a lot longer getting where you are going by stopping to look for the strays. But that's the way the people want it—and they will support it, so that in the long run that strategy gets you where you want to go a lot quicker.

Alexander the Great may have been the first military commander who sensed that you can't advance an army by leaving behind the wounded. It is something all great leaders understand. When you are a father or mother, you have to reach out to help that child who seems to be straying furthest from the family's general advance. When you are quarterbacking a football team, you learn the hard way that if you don't have the other ten players working with you, you'll be driven back every time. There can't be coalition politics on a football squad or, for very long, in a nation.

The President of the United States has to find ways of moving everyone together, or moving not at all. He's got to advance the national interest as a way of helping all the special interests, not the other way around. What's good for the United States is good for General Motors, not vice versa.

This means he's got to find ways of helping the elderly by helping the young. His administration has to design ways of helping the rich and talented and advantaged by helping the poor and helpless and weak. The poor and weak can advance by ways that also advance the rich and powerful and creative (who are the citizens who should be motivated to pull the greatest share of the burden in a general advance of the entire body politic).

What a task for a President, you may say. How difficult it seems. But there may be, as Jeffrey Bell puts it, a "simplicity that lies beyond the complexity." The pieces all seem to be there, ready to fall together. The rich and powerful and creative—a group relatively small in number—are ready to pull, if only they are not discouraged by the government from doing so. But the citizens on the other end of the scale—a group of enormous size—are the nation's most underutilized resource. Because they are so far behind, they have the most to gain in a general advance because they have the furthest to rise.

3 *Barriers to Opportunity*

I made the observation earlier that the Democratic Party, as the party inclined to redistribution, doesn't understand economic growth as well as it might. The reader has every right to ask, "So what does Jack Kemp know about economic growth? What makes you such an expert?"

These questions came up repeatedly in 1978 as the news media took a greater interest in the tax legislation I had been sponsoring in one form or another for the previous five years. I had one such exchange with a correspondent for the magazine *Politics Today*. Here is how it went:

> PT: In several interviews you've given great credit to the economists and so on, and you don't pretend, you say, to be an expert in economics; although that's now arguable, I take it.
>
> KEMP: Well, right about now I would say I'm an expert in incentive. . . . I played quarterback for about 27 of my 35 years in organized and professional football. I was president of the football players' union. I bargained collectively

on behalf of the players. I operated in an environment that was basically very marginal, to the extent that everything you do in professional football as quarterback is on the margin. You're in the huddle, you get 30 seconds, you call the play. Either it works or it doesn't. Your success is easily measurable. You have three seconds to get the ball, get back, and choose a receiver from four or five different possibilities. It's incentive. It's price theories, a reward-risk ratio. It's a thing that really is very important, at least intuitively. Then what I've done is get vitally interested in economic growth, read a great deal, try to find out what experiences the world has had and our country has had in various strategies for growth and prosperity and freedom. I have a philosophical commitment to free enterprise, to democratic capitalism, and it seems to me in reading and studying and arguing and debating and listening and talking to people, from steel workers to investors, that clearly there is a correlation between reward and effort. Once you understand that, you understand price theory. Once you understand price theory, you realize that there are only two uses of time—leisure and work. Clearly, work and saving are more important than just consumption and leisure, and a society that rewards consumption and leisure more than it rewards saving and work is a society, black or white, rich or poor, Third World or developed world, that is on the decline.

You don't have to quarterback a professional football team to become an expert in incentives, although it does sharpen your awareness of risks and rewards when on every play you have to get the job done while monsters on the opposing team are literally trying to pound you into the ground. To one degree or another, everyone is an expert in incentive, in risk-taking, in effort and reward, and in growth. I don't think there are many economists who would dispute the idea that there can't be growth without risk-taking. And by that I don't mean throwing the long ball. I mean by risk-taking the process of investment, that is, an individual's willingness to devote time, intellectual and physical energy, or financial resources to an enterprise on the chance that this effort will be rewarded in the future. In different forms, parents around the world have for ages been telling their children, as my parents told me, "You only get out of life what you put into it."

The individual who seeks instant reward, immediate self-gratification, *does not contribute to economic growth.* Unless someone in society is willing to put forth extra effort now on the chance of future payoff, there can only be *a division of current production.* What gives an economy dynamism is when most of its participants are working for future reward. Parents give up a trip to Bermuda or a bigger house or a fancy automobile in order to finance Junior's education on the chance that Junior will make good use of it. In turn, Junior gives up instant gratification in order to gain an education, forgoing the full-time low-level job that would give him the time and money here and now.

Instead of eating the seed corn, the farmer risks it in the field along with his labor, his reward coming—if drought or blight or a market collapse does not prevent it from coming at all—long after he makes this investment. Young couples incur the expense and constraints of bearing and raising children because they believe in the long-time rewards of a successful family life. The novelist or composer or playwright writes one failure after another, sharpening skills in the hope that his or her ultimate success, recognition, and reward will make it all worthwhile.

This is what growth is all about. And the reason the United States of America became the hope of the world —the "land of opportunity"—was that our government fostered a climate conducive to growth. For most of our history as a nation, the only barriers to opportunity—with the despicable exception of racial barriers—were those imposed by the earth itself. The barriers to growth were natural—mountains and deserts to be crossed, the wilderness to be cleared, the reluctance of the terrain to give up its mineral resources. But these barriers were overcome by human ingenuity, spurred by the promise of reward that would follow long after the risks were taken and the investments made. For the most part, the United States government, reflecting the collective will of its citizenry, held back its hand, and instead of staying the process of growth, actively encouraged it. The Homestead Act opened to private ownership lands held in collective trust. Enormous rewards of land were offered the private railroad companies as an inducement to quickly tie together the nation by rail.

Man-made governmental barriers to growth and opportunity have been more a feature of this century's landscape. In most cases this seems to have been a natural result of the closing of the frontier and the maturing of the economy. By this I mean the people as a whole, acting through their government, decide they must block that kind of growth which subtracts from the collective interest. Laws are passed to prevent individuals from expanding enterprises if it means they must pollute rivers or foul the air in the process. Laws are passed to prevent individual enrichment at the expense of the environment, with future as well as present generations of the citizenry in mind. Pure food and drug laws, safety laws, laws against price-fixing—all of these are the expressions of an idea held by the citizenry as a whole that individual growth that comes at the expense of the community at large must be blocked by the community at large, i.e., through the government.

Obviously, these kinds of barriers to opportunity are not those that I believe are holding us back, for the kind of growth that comes at the expense of the commonweal is not growth at all. Chopping down the redwood forests to make picnic tables is the same as eating seed corn. It is the exact opposite of investment.

The degree of regulation by government is another matter, however. The kind of man-made governmental barriers to economic growth and individual opportunity that I believe should be torn down are those which unnecessarily impede citizens from taking part in legitimate commerce which—the Declaration of Independence points out—is their natural right. Commerce is legitimate whenever individual enrichment does not injure the common good. When, as is frequently the case these days, the government passes a law or writes a regulation that unnecessarily blocks off an avenue of advance to individuals, the commonweal suffers, and the public becomes disenchanted with government.

The reason I place so much stress on the tax system as the key to spurring real economic growth is that I believe tax rates are so clearly and unnecessarily high—as the result of inflation pushing people into higher income brackets—that they stifle individual achievement *and* impoverish the community at large. I came to realize this during my first two terms as a Congressman, and to sense as well how barren traditional economic theories had become. As a freshman Congressman who had won his seat by a tiny margin, I had every incentive to search for solutions to the worst problems my constituents faced. Buffalo was one of the highest taxed, unemployed, and underemployed areas in the U.S., and, like the rest of our country, suffered from a crippling inflation. What was most discouraging, however, was listening to the arguments of most professional economists, including those who were regular advisers to the GOP. Always the advice seemed to be the same: Either accept more inflation or more unemployment. You can't solve both problems at once. In effect, they were asking me to choose among my constituents. Fight inflation to help this family, or get that father back to work at the cost of more inflation. Some choice!

There was, though, a professional economist whose statement in the national press in the autumn of 1974 caught my eye, and I felt I was onto something new and important. I used that statement by Professor Robert Mundell of Columbia University again and again in the years that followed, for it seemed to so crisply summarize our problem: "The level of U.S. taxes has become a drag on economic growth in the United States. The national economy is being choked by taxes—asphyxiated. Taxes have increased even while output has fallen, because of the inflation." Mundell, I sensed, had gotten to the heart of the problem. Inflation had been interacting with the tax system to cause real rates of taxation to increase, in the process choking down the nation's productivity.

But while this idea illuminated the problem, I was still having trouble seeing the whole picture. Because I continued to view the economy as divided between consumers and producers, I still thought that the only way to increase the nation's productivity was to lower business taxes as an inducement to greater profits and production. The taxes on labor, I thought, did not figure into the solution, because labor meant consumption. Workers, after all, were consumers, were they not? And if workers had more after-tax income they would buy more, bidding up prices and causing inflation. In retrospect, I was still thinking in Keynesian terms, and not stopping to consider that *for labor, too, greater after-tax wages translate into greater incentives to produce!* As a result of my misunderstanding, the Jobs Creation Act I designed and promoted in the 94th Congress was largely focused on cutting tax rates on capital.

It wasn't until the spring of 1976 that I came to see the deficiency in my outlook. It was pointed out to me by Jude Wanniski, then associate editor of the *Wall Street Journal*, who in turn had been shown the error by a friend of Mundell's, Professor Arthur B. Laffer of the University of Southern California's business school.

In Wanniski's book, *The Way the World Works*, published in 1978, here is how he put it:

> [Mundell and Laffer] saw the breaking down of the international monetary system having detrimental secondary effects far in excess of the primary beneficial effects alleged by the Nixon economists: for the first time in the history of civilization, a global inflation would be experienced during an era of almost universal progressivity

in national tax structures. Economic contraction would occur . . . because rates of taxation would automatically increase in the inflation, increasing government impediments to production and commerce.

There had to be, I came to realize, a balance in the tax rates paid by capital and labor. In getting this clear in my own mind, and in order to explain to others what I meant, I developed an example close to my experience—tax rates paid by a professional football team.

Starting with the notion that the more you tax something the less you get of it, and the more you subsidize something the more you get of that thing, suppose as a nation we decided it would be a good thing to have better quarterbacks on our professional football teams. One way to do this would be to pass a law absolving all pro quarterbacks from paying personal income taxes. Throughout the nation, we might imagine, fathers would encourage their sons to be quarterbacks instead of halfbacks or baseball or basketball players. As a result of this heightened competition, higher-quality quarterbacks would appear.

Carrying the example further, suppose as a nation we decided we wanted better pro football teams and more of them. Through the tax laws we could do the same, not only absolving all football players from income taxes, but also the several hundred workers associated with each enterprise—the front office, the groundskeepers, the ticket takers, vendors, and parking-lot attendants. We could then easily imagine a great multiplication of pro football teams, new leagues, and teams in any city of any size.

But suppose that at the same time the nation decided

that owners of football teams did not do any real work and so should not get any rewards for ownership, and raised their tax rate to 100 percent. We would soon find that there were no pro football teams, for no one would put the time and money into assembling the enterprise and paying the bills until money came in from ticket sales. With taxes on labor zero, and taxes on capital 100 percent, there is no enterprise at all, and thus no revenue to the government. The tax on capital is a barrier to the financial opportunity not only of owners, but also of the players and workers—and it diminishes the leisure opportunity of fans.

The same thing happens if we turn the example around, offering capital zero tax rates on profitability but piling steep tax rates on the players and workers. Potential owners would have great incentive to start teams, but they would have to pay such high salaries to workers and players to interest them in the work that fans would be discouraged by ticket prices, and teams would be possible only in the largest markets.

Now it's pretty likely that if your favorite professional sports team folded, you'd find out about it pretty quick—and be hopping mad about it. But how about if you were a machine tool operator, and instead of there being thirty factories in your city that might be able to use your skills —*as there might have been had there been greater incentives to start manufacturing there*—only fifteen places have any use for your skills? Here's something a lot more important to you than your favorite team—an increased likelihood of being without work, your skills being less in demand, your paycheck smaller—but you wouldn't even know it had happened!

The most frequent barriers to opportunity today are not "whites only" factories or businesses to which "no Irish need apply." They are factories and businesses that never were because it wasn't worth it for anyone to build them! They are the inner-city wrecks that stand empty now because their occupants couldn't afford to retool. They are the jobs that will never be because your would-be employer can't afford to pay your wages and then pay the government more in payroll taxes, unemployment insurance, Social Security charges, and the like *because* he hired you.

The combined effect of such barriers to opportunity is what Laffer calls "the wedge." Taxes on capital, taxes on labor, inflation, bureaucratic regulation, minimum wage laws, are all—to different degrees—unnecessary slices of the wedge that stand between an individual's effort and reward for that effort. Obviously, the wedge cannot be entirely removed. There must be taxes to pay for those things that require collective effort. Some regulations are essential for public health and safety. But it is the job of those in public life to find and eliminate barriers that serve no social good.

People have a hard time grasping the fact that something that seems a benevolent policy can wind up being a barrier. Minimum wage laws are a classic example of well-intentioned legislation that increases the wedge for those least in need of additional obstacles. When the minimum wage rises by law, millions of Americans see their wages increase as their employers comply with the law. To them, the increase is an unalloyed social good. George Meany, president of the AFL-CIO, even sees minimum wage legislation as the government's chief anti-poverty weapon. What these people do not realize, because it is out of their sight, is the increase in unemployment that inevitably follows an increase in the minimum wage, and that the greatest burden is being borne by black teenagers.

At least two black economists have addressed themselves to the effects of the minimum wage. Wendell W. Gunn, a former student of Laffer's, explained to the Republican Platform Committee at the 1976 GOP convention that "black teenagers, like white teenagers, could and would find work at two dollars per hour, but are prohibited by law from doing so." In that situation—or when an employer could afford to hire a young person at two dollars but not at $2.30 per hour—the minimum wage law became a total barrier to opportunity, in effect a 100 percent tax rate on black teenagers!

In a study published in 1978, Walter Williams, an associate professor of economics at Temple University, explained what groups bear the burden of the minimum wage:

> . . . the workers who bear the heaviest burden are those that are the most marginal. These are workers who employers perceive as being less productive or more costly to employ than other workers. In the U.S. labor force, there are at least two segments of the labor force who share the marginal worker characteristics to a greater extent than do other segments of the labor force. The first group consists of youths in general. They are low skilled or marginal because of their age, immaturity and lack of work experience. The second group, which contains members of the first group, are some racial minorities such as Negroes, who as a result of racial discrimination and a number of other

socioeconomic factors, are disproportionately represented among low-skill workers. These workers are not only made unemployable by the minimum wage, but their opportunities to upgrade their skills through on-the-job training are also severely limited.

In his study of the impact of a rising minimum wage on the teenage employment market, Professor Williams found what one might expect. As the minimum rose, from fifty cents an hour in 1948 to $2.30 in 1976, the general level of unemployment rose. But teenage unemployment is where you find the dramatic increases: The white teenage unemployment rate climbed from 10.2 percent in 1948 to 19.7 percent in 1976; and black teenage unemployment—lower than the rates for white teenagers until 1955—climbed from 9.4 percent in 1948 to 40.6 percent in 1976. Were the government to set the minimum wage at, say, five dollars per hour, it would succeed in unemploying nearly 100 per cent of black teenagers!

Of all the barriers to opportunity imposed by government, I can think of few more onerous than the minimum wage law, for it arrests the natural development of young people at a crucial stage. At best, the law should be removed entirely; and at the least, a separate minimum should be enacted for teenage employees. Unfortunately, there is considerable support for the law among well-meaning affluent whites who are sufficiently removed from its effects that they are unaware of its perversity.

In my experience, though, there is a difference between the political pressures for maintaining and increasing the minimum wage and those for maintaining and increasing high marginal tax rates on capital and labor.

The motives behind the minimum wage are well intentioned. George Meany and some other labor leaders argue with passion and conviction that an ever-higher minimum will effectively eliminate poverty. There is no such passion and conviction in their arguments against a lowering of unnecessarily high tax rates on capital or even on labor. The argument, simply, is that high tax rates are necessary to prevent people from making too much money. They fully recognize that when tax rates become unreasonably high, the incentive to continue producing or investing diminishes to the vanishing point and the individual's production and investment cease. Thus the Democratic Party, at least insofar as it has been dominated by the liberal-labor coalition, stands foursquare behind a minimum wage that takes the *bottom* rungs off the opportunity ladder, and just as vigorously supports maximum wage or income limits that remove the *top* rungs from the opportunity ladder. Now do you see what I meant when I said the Democratic Party has a bit to learn about economic growth?

Resistance to change of this kind, I must add, comes not only from Democrats, liberals, and labor leaders. Republicans, conservatives, and business leaders frequently seem strangely allied to the labor-liberal Democrats. Consider what happened last year when Representative William Steiger of Wisconsin introduced his amendment to lower the capital gains tax rate to 25 percent from roughly 50 percent, and put it back where it was before a Republican President boosted it in 1969. Since the higher rate so discouraged formation of new capital that the government's revenues dropped after 1969, it should have been plain to everyone involved in the tax debate of 1978 that a return to the lower rate would encourage the formation of new capital, and thus increase government revenues by increasing taxable income. But with all his might President Carter resisted the Steiger amendment—assisted by the august Business Roundtable and—to a degree—the National Association of Manufacturers as well as by the AFL-CIO and every liberal Democrat in Washington.

The conflict, I realized then, was not really between "liberals" and "conservatives." It was between the old and the new, the big and the small, those who have already made it and those at the bottom of the ladder, the "establishment" and the outsiders. Lower capital gains rates, you see, are enormous incentives to new, young, small but growing and job-creating enterprises. Most growth occurs, after all, in the young. The old and established members of the Business Roundtable and Fortune 500 have already enjoyed their great burst of youthful dynamism—the stretch of years when they were blossoming from an idea in somebody's head into a General Motors or Exxon. A slight oversimplification would be that the great resistance to the Steiger amendment came from the bureaucratic establishments of the corporate, labor, and government spheres. In any event, among the general public—as a July 1978 Roper poll showed—there was broad majority support for a lower capital gains rate.

How do we know when a specific tax rate is so high that it constitutes an unnecessary barrier to legitimate opportunity? In taxes, as in all else, there is a law of diminishing returns. When tax rates increase—as they now do automatically because of inflation—each increase has the effect of discouraging one or more individuals. They just give up trying to get ahead. I once asked a college audience the rhetorical question "What would happen if the government took New York Yankee Reggie Jackson's salary and redistributed it equally among all the Yankees?" From the back of the room came a young voice: "He'd hit singles!" And it is not only the high-income individual who decides to slack off when tax rates get too high—taking longer vacations or investing in lower-risk, lower-yield enterprises. I discovered years ago that my constituents in western New York made precise calculations about how many overtime hours it paid to work at the steel mill and how soon the amount of energy they had to expend on a Saturday shift—even at time and a half—exceeded the little bit extra that made it to their paychecks. No economist can get into the heads of the 90 million Americans in the work force and figure out precisely what the tax rates should be at any one time to raise the most revenue without stifling incentive. But when you look around and see so much evidence of unemployment and underemployment, a whole people deciding to take fewer and fewer risks, you sense that the rates today are higher than they should be. When you see more and more people shifting out of work that is visible to the tax collector and into the cash economy—the "white envelope" barter economy where taxes are not paid at all—you sense that the rates are too high, and you don't have to consult the professional economists to know that lower rates would be healthier for the economy and would likely produce greater revenues.

I believe that responding to this increasing, if subtle, despair is one of the most important tasks of politicians in the decade ahead. For some of my colleagues in public life, the most troublesome part of the project will be remembering that our constituents expect of their tax system, above all else, even-handedness. I don't want to tell you how many Republican strategists tell me we should cut taxes only for the middle class, since that, supposedly, is where "our" votes are. Forget the wealthy, forget the poor.

And my Democratic colleagues are no better with their suggestions of tax cuts for the poor—where their strategists say *their* votes are—but no cuts for the middle- and upper-income groups. It just won't work. Americans are wisely suspicious of political programs meant to divide and conquer. They rightly suspect that a system not even-handed will eventually make them, in Russell Long's words, "that guy behind the tree."

There are two other reasons why class-conscious tax cutting won't work: pride and hope. Their importance is beautifully illustrated by two anecdotes. One involves Senator George McGovern when he was the Democratic presidential nominee in 1972. Senator McGovern, an enthusiastic redistributionist, was doing fairly well in the polls until he proposed a $1000 "demogrant" to be doled out each year to persons with incomes of under $17,000. These "demogrants" would have to be financed, of course, by citizens earning more than $17,000 a year. The Senator's advisers no doubt assumed the proposal would be politically popular, because more than three-quarters of the citizenry were in the under-$17,000 category. Instead, McGovern went into a steep nosedive in the polls. After the election, I remember the defeated candidate telling newsmen, in one of the most candid admissions I've ever heard from a political leader, that the demogrant program was a mistake. "I just didn't realize," I recall him saying, "how many Americans there are who are making less than $17,000 a year who someday hope to be making more than $17,000."

Representative Abner Mikva, a Democratic colleague from Illinois, had a similar experience in his race for the House that same year, 1972, when he approached two hardhats in a suburban shopping mall to shake hands and solicit votes. Mikva says he assumed that, being hardhats, they would be friendly to a labor Democrat, but that they asked suspiciously if he favored McGovern's proposal to raise estate taxes on estates over $150,000. Because their manner indicated they didn't like the idea, Mikva asked why they didn't, since it was unlikely their estates would exceed $150,000. One of the men snapped, *"Well, someday they might!"*

4 First Things First: The Tax Strategy

It has become fashionable to dismiss almost any significant attempt to change things as "single-issue politics." Politicians, apparently, aren't supposed to emphasize anything, but are supposed to offer a big menu of small snacks. Yet when I travel around the country, I find that a single issue concerns Americans above all else: The dominant issue of our times is the anemic and unhealthy state of the U.S. economy. Tax relief is not so much an end in itself as a means of getting this economy moving again. Economic growth must come first—not because it is inherently more important than other personal and social goals, but because without growth, progress toward one goal can only be achieved by impoverishing something or someone else.

The past decade has been a marvelous learning experience. We have experimented on a vast scale with monetary vandalism, capricious redistribution of wealth, and systematic sabotage of the price system. The results have been too painfully obvious to ignore. We've rediscovered

that government cannot distribute goods that are not produced, nor can it tax activities that do not take place. We
have learned that government debt is not a source of free
wealth, and that when the supply of money outruns the
supply of things money can buy we just get more inflation.

It isn't even necessary that voters grasp the full details
of these findings, so long as markets do. When policies that
foster inflation and retard real expansion are instantly
greeted by a falling dollar, a falling stock market, and
rising interest rates, the message is not long lost on the
electorate.

In the past decade, inflation has combined with progressive tax rates to produce a growing penalty on initiative, risk, saving, and investment. More and more people
have been pushed into higher and higher tax brackets
with little or no increase in real income. The value of
standard deductions and exemptions has been diluted by
inflation. Steep taxes were imposed on wholly illusory
capital gains and interest earnings. Taxes were levied on
paper profits that failed to reflect adequately the inflated
cost of replacing plant, equipment, and inventories. The
predictable result of such demoralizing taxation is that
rapid increases in money and spending have been accompanied by virtual stagnation in real production, leaving us
with the ugly phenomenon of "stagflation."

Tax legislation throughout the decade has been inadequate to the task, and generally more concerned with
redistributing money than with fostering more production. As inflation sneakily pushed ordinary Americans into
brackets once reserved for fat cats, the congressional response has been to cut a few more taxpayers at the bottom
off the rolls. This just shifted more of the burden onto the

rest, increasing the steep progression of the tax brackets, and creating a formidable barrier to advancement. In the early 1960s, only about 3 percent of all taxable returns were subject to marginal tax rates of 30 percent or more; today, more than a third of all tax returns are in those high brackets.

In the last chapter, I mentioned Professor Arthur Laffer's "wedge." The wedge is one of Professor Laffer's contributions toward understanding the effects of government policies. Yet there is another, for which he is better known, and which bears his name—a simple, ingenious illustration of the relation between taxes and incentives.

The Laffer Curve restates the common-sense notion of diminishing returns. At some point, additional taxes so discourage the activity being taxed, such as working or investing, that they yield less revenue rather than more. There are, after all, two rates that yield the same amount of revenue: high tax rates on low production, or low rates on high production. A tax rate of 100 percent, for example, earns the same revenue as a zero tax rate—nothing —because in the first case no one would work, and in the second no taxes are collected on the income that is produced. There is, however, at any one time, some rate that allows the government maximum revenue and yet does not discourage maximum production. It is the politician's job to find out what that rate is for the time and national circumstances. A people whose nation is at war will continue to produce even when their tax rates are extremely high. In peace, tax rates must be lower—though how much depends on people's goals and aspirations, that is, on their incentives to produce.

Consider by way of example the baker who is taxed 20

percent on the first loaf of bread he and his employees bake, 40 percent on the second loaf, 60 percent on the third, 80 percent on the fourth, and 100 percent on the fifth, and who, given the level of technology in his economy, is capable of producing only one loaf of bread per day. His objective is clearly to increase his output of bread and thus increase his income. Under the tax system just described, however, his rewards for pushing forward on the frontiers of baking technology are reduced again and again for each additional loaf that he bakes. When he is at the level of four loaves—or at the margin, the 100 percent tax rate—all incentive to increase his baking productivity is ended, because if the baker were to produce a fifth loaf of bread, it would be taxed entirely away.

Or, ask yourself this question: If we had a tax whereby on the first working day the government took 10 percent of your wages, on the second day 20 percent, on the third day 30 percent, on the fourth day 40 percent, on the fifth day 50 percent, and on the sixth day 60 percent, and 70 percent on the seventh day, would you continue to work and produce on the last two or three days of the week? Not many people would. (I haven't even mentioned inflation. Increased earnings combined with a progressive tax system mean higher taxes, of course. But inflation makes it that much worse—in fact, it pushes people into higher brackets even when their real earnings haven't increased at all!)

The Laffer Curve has nothing to do with *average* tax rates for the whole economy, but instead deals with *marginal* tax rates and their effect on the economic activity of individuals. A marginal tax rate is the added tax imposed on *added* earnings. To see what I mean, let's go back to our hapless baker. He has just finished baking his fourth loaf and is trying to decide whether to bake a fifth. His first loaf was taxed at 20 percent, his second at 40 percent, the third at 60 percent, and the one he has just finished at 80 percent. His *average* tax at this point is 50 percent $[(20+40+60+80) \div 4=50]$. But if he bakes a fifth loaf, he will be taxed at 100 percent. The tax rate on his *next* loaf is the *marginal* rate, in this case, 100 percent. Our baker just decided to take a vacation!

When someone is considering starting a new business, learning a new skill, investing in stock or taking a second job, what matters is not the average tax on his or her existing earnings, *but how much of any added earnings he or she will be allowed to keep.* Without added earnings there can be no added production, and without added production there can be no growth.

The idea that lower marginal tax rates can produce higher tax revenues seems too good to be true to some people. It seems to promise something for nothing. Indeed, the whole line of reasoning is not readily accepted, or even fully understood, by the older economics establishment of either political party. (After all, the argument for supply-side fiscal policy essentially repudiates Keynesian "demand management," which has been the fundamental operating principle of the past decade. To admit that the older principle was wrong, many economists would have to acknowledge some responsibility for the miserable state of the economy. They might even have to recall their textbooks!)

Actually, economics is, in a sense, the science of how to get more with less. That's what we mean by improved productivity or efficiency. But "more" isn't just tons of steel or numbers of widgets; it is just as much a matter of quality as quantity. A strong economy produces not only more goods, but better goods.

The ultimate source of improved productivity is always human ingenuity. It isn't just amazing inventors like Edison or dramatic managerial innovators like Henry Ford. Improvements in efficiency spring from millions of creative workers, supervisors, and managers whose intimate knowledge of their tasks leads to new methods of improving products or saving costs. From this vast pool of dispersed knowledge, a market economy draws people who gamble that they have a better idea about how to provide more or better goods with fewer or cheaper resources. But they won't take those risks unless they will be rewarded if they succeed. By continually removing the incentives which reward achievement, we have created a system which taxes the imagination, ingenuity, and enterprise of the American people.

Last year, the Joint Budget Committees put out a pamphlet entitled *Leading Economists' Views of Kemp-Roth,* referring to the tax-rate-reduction bill Senator Roth and I sponsored. The definition of "leading economist," pretty much restricted membership to those who had served on the Council of Economic Advisers while the economy slid into decay, or those whose econometric models have consistently failed to predict turns toward inflation, recession, or both. There were, however, some thoughtful criticisms in the Budget Committee pamphlet that merit an answer, although they are sometimes obscured by intemperate language. (MIT Professor Robert Solow's scholarly judgment is that our views constitute "media hype" and "snake oil.")

The easiest objections to dismiss are the elaborate statistical or "econometric" projections of what would happen under alternative tax policies. Chase Econometrics boldly forecasts the effect of Kemp-Roth all the way to 1987. Wharton's model tells us that Kemp-Roth would make inflation in 1980 precisely $19/100$ of 1 percent higher than otherwise. Despite the spurious illusion of precision, this is just pretending to knowledge that the forecasters do not have. The econometric models have trouble predicting the next quarter much less the next decade.

"The trouble with these exercises," says the Citibank monthly economic letter, "is that they miss the point. What Laffer is talking about is a change in real GNP produced by a shift in supply rather than in demand. The large econometric models are simply not designed to answer the subtle question of what happens when incentives to produce are increased."

If you don't ask computers the right questions, they can't give the right answers. Data Resources says, "No direct labor supply effect is found for the tax cuts." *But no such effect could possibly be "found," because the DRI computer*—according to DRI president Otto Eckstein, "does not include a tax term in its supply of labor equation"—*has been programmed to assume that marginal tax rates have no effect whatsoever on the incentive to work.*

One excuse for that strange assumption is a footnote reference to some suspiciously archaic studies of executive behavior (dated 1951, 1957, 1966, and 1970). More recent research by one of the same authors cited by DRI, Professor George Break of the University of California, Berkeley, suggests that a 10 percent increase in after-tax pay increases the quantity of work by about 4 percent (and much more than that for wives, elderly workers, and teenagers). But there is more to effort than the number of bodies putting in hours. Professor Paul Taubman of the University of Pennsylvania points out that "high tax rates may induce people to expend less effort on the job and to avoid positions with great burdens and responsibilities," or "to substitute home production for goods worked for and bought in the marketplace."

Data Resources also claims that experiments with negative income taxes—cash payments to those with low incomes—show that "the effects are small or nonexistent." That is flatly untrue. In the New Jersey experiment, white male household heads worked five to seven hours a week less if they received payments. In the Rural Income Maintenance Experiment, "38 percent fewer Iowa wives worked." In the Seattle-Denver study, there was a 61 percent increase in family break-up, and a reduction in hours of work that ranged from 5 percent for male family heads to 22 percent for wives.

So, common sense again prevails, and we are left with the ancient dilemma of motivating people with either the carrot of take-home pay or the stick of potential deprivation. The Soviet Union prefers the stick: unemployment is considered a crime ("parasitism") punishable by a year in prison, and pension and welfare benefits—when available at all—are at near-starvation levels. This country is far more compassionate, refraining from spurring people with the stick of dire need. But that is all the more reason why we must not tax away the carrot.

There is yet another incentive argument for lower tax rates yielding more revenue: *With lower tax rates there is, to put it bluntly, less incentive to cheat.* While we haven't yet reached the wholesale tax evasion of some European countries, the "underground" economy is nonetheless growing rapidly.

Professor Peter Gutmann of Baruch College was intrigued by the suspiciously huge rise in the use of currency (the number of $100 bills in circulation rose 250 percent from 1967 to mid-1978); he estimated that all that green stuff financed a tax-free "subterranean" cash economy of almost $200 billion in 1977. Even if we assume, conservatively, an average federal and state tax of only 30 percent, some $60 billion (30 percent of $200 billion) in revenue could be gained by minimizing the current incentives for tax avoidance and evasion.

The symptoms of growing tax avoidance are all too obvious: the home repairman who insists on being paid in cash, the brokers' listings that openly boast that a tavern earns more than its books show—that sort of thing. Occasional IRS in-depth audits show a sizable decline in compliance among small businesses, while households refusing to disclose sources of income to census officials rose from 10.2 percent in 1972 to 19.5 percent in 1976. When workers are illegal aliens, both the employer and employee avoid the payroll tax wedge—and one or two million foreign workers probably evade the eye of the tax collector in this way. Recently, two researchers at the University of Michigan, Louis Ferman and Louise Brandt, found that nearly a fourth of all home-related services (painting, plumbing, etc.) came from the underground economy.

While the initial reaction might be to "crack down on cheaters," that never works when the incentives for tax avoidance are powerful and widespread. Remaining taxpayers just end up paying the salaries of thousands more tax collectors. *What is needed instead is to reduce the tax penalty for being honest.*

Although the main effect of tax cuts in enlarging tax revenues comes from incentives, there are many other favorable effects on the economy and tax base. When marginal tax rates are excessive there is widespread underreporting of income, greater payment in tax-free "perks," wasteful use of resources (lawyers' services, tax shelters) to escape taxes, more early retirement, more do-it-yourself projects and barter to avoid efficient (but taxable) specialization, and so on. There is no way to know precisely how much of a revenue loss all this amounts to, nor the extent to which it is a drag on the economy. Professor Herbert Stein, when asked about the importance of such effects, answered with honorable candor, "I don't know the answer to many of those questions." But he then advised the Budget Committee to "base its decisions on things we know with reasonable confidence." That would be reasonable and prudent if one could assume that continuing on our present course is safer than testing uncharted waters. But our present course has created much misery and fear, and there is little hope for a change in results without a change in policy.

We have tried what the mainstream economists thought they knew, and it simply didn't work. Yet we are still being told that austerity is the only cure for inflation, and that inflation is the only sure cure for stagnation. The American people have enough sense of history to realize that is no choice at all. We do not have to choose between the recession of 1975 and the unhealthy inflation of the past two years. Of that there *is* proof.

Two historical precedents show what a growth-oriented tax strategy can accomplish. In the 1920s, beginning in 1922, tax rates were cut five times—from a range of 4 percent to 73 percent in 1920 to a range of 0.4 percent to 24 percent by 1929. Production and employment soared, and the much lower tax rates brought in more tax revenues. Real output grew by 4.7 percent a year from 1922 to 1929. The number of taxpayers reporting incomes of more than $50,000 tripled between 1920 and 1928, so that lower rates on high incomes generated twice as much revenue.

"Experience does not show that the higher rate produces the larger revenue," said President Coolidge. "Experience is all in the other way. . . . There is no escaping the fact that when the taxation of large incomes is excessive, they tend to disappear."

"The much-maligned Coolidge era," wrote Alan Reynolds in *The Public Interest,* "provided five years of 3.5 percent unemployment and 0.5 percent inflation—a combination that is impossible in Keynesian theory (especially with budget surpluses), and certainly unmatched in Keynesian practice."

The second major experiment with a growth-oriented tax reduction occurred between 1962 and 1965, begun under the administration of President John F. Kennedy. Kennedy's plan was to cut personal tax rates about 30 percent across the board, lowering the maximum rate from 91 to 70 percent and the minimum rate from 20 to 14 percent, with additional reductions in business taxes. The tax cuts not only forestalled a widely anticipated recession, but launched the economy on a prolonged period of prosperity, interrupted only by a loose monetary policy and a tax surcharge later in the decade. We completed the entire decade without a single recession. Inflation didn't exceed 3 percent until 1968, despite an intensity of use of manufacturing capacity (over 91 percent in 1966) and a rate of unemployment (3.8 percent) now regarded as impossible, or wildly inflationary.

I should mention that our view that the Kennedy tax cuts worked mainly by unleashing private incentives on the supply side has been challenged by Professor Walter Heller, who was Chairman of the Council of Economic Advisers at the time. "The record is crystal clear that it was its stimulus to *demand* . . . that powered the 1964–65 expansion . . . it drew on 'aggregate supply' capacity that already existed." According to Professor Heller, "To give any credence to the Kemp-Roth thesis that the 1964 tax cut accomplished all this by unleashing incentive and triggering a great leap forward on the supply side, one would have to find a sudden bulge in productivity and GNP potential in the economic statistics for the mid-1960s. No such bulge occurred."

Well, let's take a look. The number of people working or seeking work increased by only 660,000 per year from 1957 through 1962, but by over 1.3 million a year from 1963 through 1968. That wasn't just using workers who were already willing to work. Real business investment hovered below 9 percent of GNP from 1958 through 1963, but jumped to 9.3 percent in 1964 and averaged 10.4 percent of GNP from 1965 through 1969. That wasn't just using up existing equipment. Productivity in private business increased by an unprecedented rate of more than 3.9 percent per year for the five years from 1962 through 1966. If that wasn't a "bulge" in productivity, I don't know what is.

What about government revenues? Did this tax relief spell the end of programs for the indigent? Quite the contrary! *Though federal tax receipts increased by only 18 percent from 1957 to 1962, they soared by more than 50 percent from 1962 to 1967, under the prospect and reality of lower rates.* And that startling revenue effect can't be attributed to soaring inflation, which averaged 1.6 percent per year in the earlier period and only imperceptibly higher (2.3 percent) in 1962–1967.

Contrary to Professor Heller's belief, growth of "demand" or total spending was at only about half the pace of the previous two years. The difference was that growth of spending in the 1960s was met by comparable increases in production, while today's far faster growth of demand just brings more inflation.

In short, Professor Heller deserves credit for doing the right thing, even if he did it for the wrong reason. His error, like that of many critics of Kemp-Roth, has been to ignore the crucial distinction between marginal tax rates affecting individual choices, and average tax rates. That is, they miss the whole point.

Michael Evans of Chase Econometrics, an astute and generally sympathetic critic, points out that "the proportion of Federal personal income taxes to total personal income or of total Federal government receipts to total GNP has remained almost constant over the last quarter-century." That statement about average receipts tells us nothing about marginal rates. And it is misleading even on its own terms. The share of personal income coming from government salaries and transfer payments has risen very sharply, so expressing taxes as a percentage of personal income understates the burden on private workers and firms.

Several other critics point to the higher average tax revenues in some other countries that nonetheless have experienced fairly brisk expansion. Again, this confuses average tax revenues with marginal tax rates. European countries rely heavily on flat-rate sales (VAT, value-added tax) and payroll taxes, so that marginal tax rates on added earnings are lower than ours even though average tax revenues are higher. (In Japan, of course, even the average tax is much lower.) United States governments, at all levels, get 45 percent of their revenues from the income tax; that compares with 33 percent in Germany and 29 percent in Norway. Germany's top tax rate is 50 percent; ours is 70 percent at the federal level alone (and up to 19 percent in state and local income taxes). Germany imposes no capital gains tax at all.

Professor Herbert Stein comes a little closer to the mark. He calculates that the average marginal tax rate from all taxes was 38 percent—that is, if the economy produced another dollar of output, thirty-eight cents would go to taxes. Kemp-Roth would cut that to thirty-three cents. But the nation as a whole does not face a marginal tax rate; individuals do. It makes little sense to ask if marginal tax rates are, *on the average,* discouragingly high. Half of the people might face marginal tax rates of less than 38 percent, and half might face rates above 38 percent, *yet a significant portion could still face marginal rates of 100 percent or even more.*

Numerous studies show, for example, that after-tax income can easily be *reduced* by giving up a package of tax-free welfare, unemployment, or disability benefits and taking a job. That is equivalent to a marginal tax rate of over 100 percent—you *lose* money by working more.

A 70 percent rate on earnings from dividends or interest that don't even keep up with inflation, not to mention state income taxes, can easily exceed 100 percent of the gain in *real* income. And there is ample evidence that the tax on inflated capital gains has been hugely confiscatory —levying taxes on what were really capital losses before inflation.

The Kemp-Roth tax bill is sometimes depicted as drastic or wildly inflationary—starving the Treasury for funds and straining the economy's capacity. Accepting the Treasury's estimates uncritically, some journalists have concluded that the alleged revenue loss of $112 billion by 1981 would create massive budget deficits, and that those deficits would so stimulate nominal GNP growth they would fuel even more inflation. *Business Week* threatened flamboyantly that Kemp-Roth would "generate an inflation that would destroy the value of the currency."

The fundamental problem with Treasury revenue estimates is that they are entirely static. *They assume that people pay no attention to tax rates.* In *Federal Tax Reform,* recently published by the Institute for Contemporary Studies, Professor Michael Boskin points out that the Treasury's revenue estimates simply assume "that every firm and every household will continue behaving in exactly the same way before the imposition of the tax reform as they would after the tax change. . . . Therefore, when Congress is presented information about the likely effects of tax policies . . . the deck is stacked against proposals which temporarily decrease tax revenues but stimulate the long-term growth of the economy."

Even if we pretend, as the Treasury does, that tax rates don't affect behavior—the choice between consuming and saving, between work and leisure, and between risky or safe investing—the Treasury's revenue loss estimates are still about $47 billion too high in the third year. The Treasury generously assumes that nominal GNP will grow by 12 percent a year and that each 1 percent increase in nominal GNP (mostly inflation) will give them a 1.67 percent increase in revenue. *Those high estimates mean that individuals are pushed into higher brackets very rapidly, so the "loss" of revenues from Kemp-Roth really means the failure of government to profit so much from inflation.*

Let's suppose for the sake of argument that ever-increasing marginal tax rates can continue to produce more revenue. Federal tax receipts were 17.8 percent of GNP in 1965, about 19.6 percent in 1978. The 1979 budget estimated that revenues would rise to 22.8 percent of GNP by 1983, or 21.3 percent with the administration's so-called tax-reduction proposals. The percentage would be even higher were it not for the incredible assumption that real GNP would increase 4.7 percent per year from 1979 to 1983, despite rising effective tax rates. Those who talk about "lost revenues" from Kemp-Roth should be honest enough to tell us that they really mean that taxes would otherwise claim a much larger share of our incomes.

The Kemp-Roth bill would gradually reduce tax rates by one-third over three years. This would have reduced taxes in 1979 for a $17,500 family by $653. Under Kemp-Roth, the 1979 taxes for a family earning $20,000 would be reduced by $792; a family earning $30,000 would receive a $1,451 reduction.

Those who oppose these tax-rate cuts of Kemp-Roth are

really supporting the enormous tax increases that will otherwise occur. As it is, if federal revenues in 1983 took the same share of GNP as in 1965 they would be $121 billion less than projected by the 1979 Carter tax proposals.

In the following chapters, I will have much more to say about inflation and government spending. For now, let the Citibank *Monthly Economic Letter* explain how tax rate reductions will help to lower inflation. "Any possible stimulative effect of a tax cut on aggregate demand," wrote the Citibank economists, "could easily be offset by reducing the growth of the money supply. And if a tax cut were completely offset so that it had no effect on aggregate demand, the reduction in taxes could even be deflationary as the increase in the incentive to produce boosted the supply of goods relative to demand."

A number of other distinguished economists from the cautious world of business and banking are likewise not at all worried that Kemp-Roth would be inflationary. Yet some academics and journalists still insist that tax cuts cannot increase output because there is no spare capacity. In the short run, however, the improved business climate would make it profitable to use marginal existing equipment that is currently idle because it cannot be used except at a loss, and also to use other equipment more vigorously. Additional shifts likewise become feasible when they become profitable. Within a few years, new manufacturing capacity would come from more savings invested more efficiently.

In the labor market, additional capacity comes from overtime, moonlighting, working harder and better, more family members working, less work in the underground economy, less extended unemployment, less early retirement, and so on. Capacity is not "given," but depends on the rewards for using it. And capacity is not simply a fixed quantity but has a qualitative dimension as well. We can work better as well as longer, we can invest more productively as well as investing more.

Professor Walter Heller argues that this is not the right time for a tax cut because there isn't enough spare capacity. But then he also thought that 1973 wasn't the right time for monetary restraint because there was plenty of spare capacity. We were lulled into tolerating excessive growth of money in 1972–73, and again in 1977–78, by the seductive promise that spare capacity would protect us from the inflationary consequences. It didn't.

What about business taxes, and the anemic investment in plant and equipment? Many critics of Kemp-Roth agree with Michael Evans of Chase Econometrics that "Kemp-Roth appears to be unduly balanced toward the individual as opposed to the business sector." But individuals are the ultimate source of most new investment funds (corporations owe more than they own, households do not). And the personal income tax obviously affects income from investments—dividends, interest earnings, and capital gains.

Business taxes are, of course, paid by people too. But confining most tax relief to retained corporate profits, through such devices as accelerated depreciation or an investment tax credit, keeps capital locked into established firms. By focusing on the individual investor, on the other hand, we can stimulate risk investment in innovative new firms that are the main source of new products and new techniques. New firms may have small current profits because of the high cost of growing, yet have great long-term potential if they can acquire outside funds for expansion. Cutting the profits tax won't help much if there are little or no profits, nor if the lower tax at the corporate level just results in higher taxes on the dividends and capital gains of stockholders. We instead need to give investors an incentive to buy shares of companies with low current dividends but good, though risky, potential for growth. That means a lower tax rate on capital gains of the sort boldly proposed by Representatives Steiger and Archer, but fumbled by Congress under the threat of a presidential veto.

Until 1969, the tax on long-term capital gains was effectively half of an individual's marginal tax rate, up to a maximum rate of 25 percent. Changes in the tax laws since 1969 later subjected about 40 percent of all realized capital gains to rates above 25 percent (up to a theoretical maximum of 49.1 percent), and imposed much higher rates on real, inflation-adjusted capital gains. Actual revenues from the higher tax rates fell sharply, and have yet to reach the 1968 level.

A central issue in the debate over capital gains tax rates has been their effect on the decision to buy and sell assets, such as stocks and bonds, and thus become subject to the capital gains tax. Treasury estimates of the revenue loss from a lower rate simply assume that people would realize and report the same amount of capital gains regardless of the tax rate. Yet capital gains taxes can easily be avoided by not selling the assets that you own and by not investing in such assets in the first place.

Some formidable evidence on the subject was provided

by a pair of studies for the National Bureau of Economic Research by Professors Martin Feldstein and Joel Slemrod of Harvard. Among other things, these studies estimated that limiting the long-term capital gains tax rate to 25 percent "causes a nearly threefold increase in realized gains," so that the tax revenues would have more than doubled if the tax rate had been limited to 25 percent. Feldstein and Slemrod also found that "individuals paid capital gains tax on more than $4.5 billion of nominal capital gains on corporate stock in 1973. If the costs of these shares are adjusted for increases in the consumer price level since they were purchased, the $4.5 billion nominal gain becomes a real capital loss of nearly $1 billion."

Too often today investment money is "locked in" to inefficient investments because people don't want to sell out and pay high taxes on paper profits. One significant gain from reducing the tax bias against realizing paper gains therefore would be the freeing up of these assets and creation of a more efficient capital market. Funds would move more quickly into investments yielding the best return, and investments that yield the best profit do so because consumers value those uses of resources most highly.

Another gain from the improved prospect of after-tax rewards from investing would be to increase personal (and business) saving and investment. As a recent study by Stanford Professor Michael Boskin demonstrates, savings are highly responsive to the real, after-tax return.

The administration's primary objection to reducing the maximum capital gains tax rate was that most of the benefit would accrue to "high income" individuals. If an older couple, though not yet fifty-five, with a $20,000 income decide to sell their $80,000 house and rent an apartment, for example, their income in that year could easily exceed $100,000 because the one-time capital gain was included in the administration's curious definition of income. The same is true of stocks.

If a stock rises 60 percent in ten years during which inflation averages 6 percent a year, even a 25 percent tax on that nominal gain leaves the stockholder 25 percent worse off in real terms (aside from dividends) than if he had never made the investment. Profit figures also understate the replacement cost of equipment and inventories during inflation, so taxation of real profits is increased. Since inflation pushes individuals into higher tax brackets, that portion of profits paid out as dividends is also double-taxed at increasingly steep marginal rates. Although tax rates have been periodically adjusted to partly reflect inflation, that has not been the recent experience in the higher brackets, where most personal investment takes place. In all of these ways and more, the individual investor has suffered badly from inflation and taxes. A look at the trends suggests he's an endangered species.

For example, we desperately need to get the individual back into the stock market. Pension fund trustees are not even allowed (much less motivated) to make the kinds of risky investments needed to promote change. In 1964, private investors did 65 percent of the trading on the New York Stock Exchange; now they do less than 30 percent. The reason is no secret. Lawrence Fisher and James Lorie of the University of Chicago calculate that the annual real rate of return on stocks (dividends and capital gains) was *minus* 6.2 percent from 1972 through 1976—*just slightly*

*better than the minus 6.6 percent real annual decline
from 1929 to 1933!*

Stock prices are both a cause and an effect of economic
prosperity—a barometer of the expected value of the nation's accumulated capital. Research by James Tobin of
Yale shows that business will not make new investments
in a weak stock market, because the market is signaling
that those investments aren't likely to pay off. Research by
Barry Bosworth, currently director of the Council on
Wage and Price Stability, indicates that a fourth of the
decline in real output during the last recession was caused
by the previous loss of wealth of stockholders. It is impossible to have a strong economy when the stock market is
weak, and the market's judgment on the value of public
policy initiatives must be constantly monitored and re-
spected.

In the final days of the 95th Congress, the market
sagged sharply on news of disappointing tax legislation
and a downright destructive energy bill. It plummeted
under the official endorsement of perpetual inflation that
passed for the administration's "anti-inflation" scheme.
Altogether, the value of the nation's capital stock, as measured on the New York Stock Exchange, lost over $110
billion in the space of two weeks, before taking some
encouragement from the Federal Reserve's modest ges-
tures toward monetary sanity. Indeed, the market and the
dollar have lost ground more or less continuously with
every policy move of the Carter administration. Yet the
chairman of the Council of Economic Advisers had the
audacity to appear on NBC's *Face the Nation* in May 1978
and proclaim, "Most of the bad news is in the financial
world. . . . We are principally interested in, and our princi-

pal weapons are directed toward, improving the real world."

The capital gains legislation that finally emerged from the 95th Congress was far from adequate—major reform efforts were stymied by the threat of a presidential veto. The serious problem of taxing unreal, illusory, inflated gains—the "indexing" issue the administration opposed and on which it would not bend—remains an urgent item for reform. Indexing is a way to prevent taxing unreal, "paper" gains—and it is desperately needed to squelch a growing possibility of public confiscation of private capital —something we call "expropriation" when it happens abroad.

The politics of envy are often inflamed by arguments that conveniently ignore the fact that without the pay we would not have the production. Income is not just there waiting to be spread around however the politicians please. Income is a flow of goods and services that must be adequately rewarded or it will cease to happen.

Professor Lester Thurow, writing in *Newsweek*, mentioned a Common Market estimate that "the richest 10 percent of our households receive 26.1 percent of our [*sic*] income." He then went on to argue that such inequality isn't necessary to achieve growth, citing Germany and Japan as examples. Unfortunately, Professor Thurow neglected to mention that the same study shows that the richest 10 percent of Japanese households produce and earn 27.8 percent of that nation's income; in Germany the top 10 percent get 30.6 percent.

Actually, the main reasons for differences in family income are the age of the household head (young trainees and older retired people earn less than experienced workers), and the number of workers in the family. In 1976, the median income for families with four workers was $25,696, with two workers it was $17,341, with no workers it was $5,689. It is not possible to erase such differences while preserving any incentive to work.

Although those with incomes above $50,000 accounted for only 1.4 percent of all taxpayers in 1976, they paid over 23 percent of all federal income taxes. The impression that high-income families escape taxation is simply false.

If anyone nonetheless wants to "soak the rich," we had better leave some of them around to tax. Although the figures are not precisely comparable, it is revealing that while 38.7 percent of all families earned over $15,000 in 1967, and could therefore afford to live on the level of the Bureau of Labor Statistics' "higher" family budget, only 17.8 percent of all families earned the equivalent income of $25,000 or more in 1976. The nation is either running out of "rich" people to tax or is taxing them into a lower standard of living.

The Coolidge tax cuts doubled the revenues from those earning over $50,000. The Kennedy tax cuts (as Michael Evans has shown) turned around a previous decline in taxes extracted from the over-$100,000 group, yielding a 49 percent increase from 1963 to 1966. Discouraging people from getting rich is no way to get taxes from rich people! The point was made superbly in a classic *Wall Street Journal* editorial entitled "Tax the Rich!"

> Consider what would happen to a "good" rich person who refuses to use loopholes and prefers hard work to sailing yachts. He decides to invest $1 million of his capital

in a widget factory in New York City, which will employ hundreds. He will run it himself, arranging the financing, assembling the personnel, finding the markets, and so forth. Give him a year to get off the ground, but say he is lucky enough in the second year to make a 10% profit on his invested capital. This is after his workers have paid federal, state and local income taxes and the widget company has paid property taxes, license fees, etc.

Of the $100,000 profit, the city clears away roughly $5,-700, leaving $94,300. The state clears away about 10% of that, leaving $84,870. The IRS, levying at progressive rates, snatches $38,000, leaving $46,870. Our good rich person then pays this to himself as a dividend.

Being rich, our man is of course in the highest personal income-tax brackets, and after paying 4.3% to the city ($2,015) has $44,855 left. The state clips him for 15% of that ($6,728) and leaves him $38,127. Uncle Sam "nicks" him for 70% of that, which is $26,689, leaving him with $11,438.

Thus, on the investment of $1 million in capital and two years hard work in assembling an enterprise that is risky to begin with, this lucky fellow who turned a profit of $100,000 has $11,438 to spend. He has given up two years on his yacht to gain $5,719 in annual income. If he had invested in tax-free municipals, he would have gained roughly $60,000 in annual income and could have remained on his yacht instead of fighting New York City traffic, City Hall, and the widgetmakers union.

When you knock Brown down a few rungs from his top perch on the ladder, Smith has to give way below him, too; but Jones, who was clinging to the bottom rung, is pushed off entirely. Once we get past the idea that taxing the rich into earning less somehow benefits society as a whole, we can start putting rungs back on the economic ladder and get everyone climbing again.

Death taxes are another government device which manages to confiscate property without getting much revenue to show for it. Death taxes have a rather checkered history. The federal government first imposed an inheritance tax during the Civil and Spanish-American Wars to raise emergency revenues—then enacted the current estate tax in 1916 on the eve of American involvement in the war in Europe. A gift tax was first tried experimentally in the flush years of 1924 and 1925—but discarded because it was too complicated for the amount of revenue it raised. The same could be said of the current gift tax, which was made permanent by Herbert Hoover in 1932.

Today, the combined federal gift and estate tax, and the states' inheritance taxes, are justified on the basis of that familiar static assumption that there is only so much wealth to go around. When somebody dies, this idea says, you break up his estate and throw it back into the pot, or else no one else can accumulate an estate. Yet selling the family business or farm to pay the estate taxes does not strike me as the way to increase the general welfare—and that's exactly what's happening all across the country. We tax gifts and estates with rates ranging from 18 percent to 70 percent—almost the same as income. Surviving spouses must look for protection to exemptions and exclusions which are worth less each year because of inflation. Orphans receive little special protection. Children have to pay the same rates as unrelated inheritors, and a 1976 change in the law removed the tax benefits for grandchildren of "generation-skipping" trusts.

The prospect of providing security for one's heirs was once a powerful motive for continuing to work up to potential in the later years of life. With that incentive gone, retirement age is drifting down to fifty-five in many industries. And both the early retiree and his or her dependents are more likely to end up dependent on the taxpayer rather than on the earnings from accumulated savings invested in a growing economy.

The understandable result of the uncertainties of passing on one's holdings after death is that there are relatively fewer estates to tax. Gift and estate taxes accounted for only 1.7 percent of federal revenue in 1976, compared with 4.4 percent in 1941.

West Germany has an idea which I believe would improve both the fairness and efficiency of death taxes in the United States. Instead of an estate tax, there is an inheritance tax which is graduated according to how closely related the inheritor is to the deceased. There are four groups: spouses, children, and orphaned grandchildren; grandchildren and their descendents; parents, grandparents, siblings, and in-laws; and all others. The first group pays tax rates which are only half as large as the fourth, with the other two tax tables in between. This system seems to provide a better break than ours for close relations beyond spouses.

If the United States adopted such a system, inheritors should continue to receive a tax credit for state inheritance taxes. I believe the exclusion of most life insurance policies, which was in effect from 1918 to 1941, should also be revived. If there is more assurance that a person can transfer his estate to his intended heirs, I have no doubt whatsoever that there will be more estates to transfer, and that with lower effective tax rates revenue would increase from the paltry 1 percent share expected in 1981.

Much of the debate between supporters and critics of Kemp-Roth reflects our different time horizons. My own concern is not with "fine tuning" taxes on an annual basis in order to achieve some immediate target rate of growth, unemployment, or inflation. Experience shows that we don't have the wisdom to do that. What government can do is to provide an environment conducive to long-term expansion of production and productivity. That requires making the sort of commitment to the future that Kemp-Roth's three-year phased tax cut implies—a commitment that people can plan on. If we continue to listen to the same aging voices that led us into our current predicament, and continue to follow slavishly their notoriously inaccurate computer models, we can look forward to another decade like the last.

Inflation is simply too much money and not enough production. Period. Real growth is a matter of individual initiative responding to incentives. Tax incentives can and must be combined with appropriate monetary discipline to eliminate inflation and lay the groundwork for sustained expansion. It is time the lessons of the past decade were put to use.

5 *The Safety Net and Government Spending*

In the last several years, time and again I have heard journalists, academics, and public officials of both parties comment with amusement on a paradox of American political life. Without fail, public opinion polls show that Americans believe taxes are too high *and* that social services should not be reduced. The polls invariably show that people have less and less confidence in government, and yet, come November, they elect the politicians and the political party which legislates bigger and bigger government. As a result, federal spending, which controlled 18 percent of the nation's production in 1965, controlled 23 percent in 1978 (not counting federal activities outside the budget or the enormous effects of government regulation).

Reactions to tax-rate reduction efforts, such as Kemp-Roth, frequently reflect these anomalies. At one and the same time, the proponents of tax reduction are suspected of attempting to undermine social services (for tax cuts mean revenue losses to those who don't understand growth), and accused of profligacy by those who insist that cuts in government spending must precede cuts in taxes! Indeed, politicians are usually pigeonholed according to where it is they put their stress. New ideas get short shrift because they don't quite fit the jargon of the day, and in not too long the habits of politics drift away from the desires of the citizenry.

The seeming dichotomies in voter preferences aren't all that hard to figure out. In a stifled economic climate, desiring lower taxes and the maintenance of social services makes perfect sense. But that is not to say that Americans want to have to spend hundreds of billions of dollars on a vast array of public services per se—as though public services had somehow become an end in themselves.

Americans have two complementary desires. They want an open, promising ladder of opportunity. And they want a safety net of social services to catch and comfort those less fortunate than themselves and those unable to share in the productive processes when the economy goes sour.

The American people consider themselves a kind of extended family. I suspect it is because so many of us are descended from people who fled suffering abroad or who arrived here "down and out" that we consciously and actively seek to aid those who need our special care. We are repelled by the thought of ignoring genuine suffering.

Yet because people want this safety net in place, it doesn't follow that they therefore want it filled up with sufferers. Least of all do they want their assistance to seduce others into habits of dependency. Rather, they want the type of economic expansion that will extend hope throughout the national family, supplying resources to aid those who need our care, and opportunity to those who now accept aid but could do, and ought to be doing, otherwise.

It seems to me the proper solution to the growing burden of social spending, then, is not to lower the safety net so far that it bounces against the ground, by slashing social-support programs. Instead, we must draw people out of the net by expanding attractive opportunities in the private sector. A vibrant economy can afford to leave the safety net in place and at the same time ensure that the net is as empty as possible.

In a stagnant, unstable economy, the demand for social services grows as the economy's ability to pay for such services contracts. Farmers demand price supports to help them cope with inflated costs and taxes, while urban consumers demand food stamps to help them pay the resulting higher food prices. We tax rural areas to fix urban decay and mass transit; we tax urban areas to pay for farm subsidies and rural electricity. We tax business to pay for benefits to unemployed workers; we tax workers to pay for subsidies to keep business afloat. Opportunities then become greater in special-interest lobbying than in producing. The whole process seems to degenerate into a scramble to see who can get the largest slices of a shrinking pie. Nobody wins in this game.

Real economic expansion is the surest remedy for this divisive sport of mutual plunder. We can't progress as a society by using government to diminish one another. The only way we can all have more is by producing more, not by bickering over how to share less. Economic growth must come first, I believe, for when it does many social problems tend to take care of themselves, and the problems that remain become more manageable.

The orthodox conservatives are stuck with a chicken-and-egg dilemma. They insist on cutting spending first and taxes second. But they have been saying this for decades, and the result is that spending and taxes have soared. Unable to sell spending cuts to the public, which does not want to initiate "growth" at the expense of social services, this group is left with no option but opposing tax-rate reduction.

We have to break out of this vicious circle where it is the most vulnerable—by lifting the tax penalty on added effort and efficiency. Our people don't want to cut social spending when the economy is stagnant, adding austerity in public services to scarcity in private goods. It is ridiculous to think that economic expansion can come at the expense of the weak. It can only come by inviting the strongest, ablest members of society to pull harder by rewarding, not punishing, them for their efforts.

A prosperous, innovative private economy competes with a bloated public sector in many ways. The most obvious is that private employment and investment opportunities become more attractive than tax-financed jobs, benefits, or subsidies. In a highly taxed economy, many more people with marginal disabilities apparently find the tax-free benefits more attractive than available opportunities to earn taxable income. There were, for example, a million more people receiving disability benefits in 1977 than in 1972. A decade ago, twice as many recipients of disability benefits returned to work as do today. With more and better opportunities, and reduced taxation of added earnings, some of the 4.8 million people drawing

$13 billion in federal disability benefits would be attracted back into the work force. Similar effects would be registered from unemployment and welfare benefits. And the 625,000 people now stuck in temporary dead-end "public-service jobs" would drop their rakes and rush to a variety of promising options. The $11.3 billion CETA program would shrink from an inability to attract applicants.

Many of my conservative colleagues despair over the prospects of pulling people out of the safety net, getting them off welfare. They fear that benefit levels have gotten so high that non-work has become permanently more attractive than work for many people. In other words, when people get $120 per week in welfare, food stamps, housing, and health-care benefits while out of work, and could get only a bit more if employed, it does suggest the implausibility of moving great numbers of people from non-work to work.

This, though, strikes me as static analysis. It is true that between losing government benefits and paying taxes on earnings, a typical family on welfare can face a marginal tax rate exceeding 100 percent for working. But it runs against human nature to actively contemplate a lifetime on the dole, and I can't recall ever meeting anyone who seriously expressed that preference. It's human nature to want more, and when individuals who are on a $120 weekly dole see a real opportunity ladder that could take them to income levels several times that amount, they will make the decision to try, even though at first they will not be better off financially. They invest in their own futures the way we all do when we see a real chance of future reward. They only choose to stay on the dole when they see little or no prospect of future advance, which is the case when the economy is in contraction.

Of all Americans, blacks are trapped deepest in the safety net, because they have carried the added burden of racial discrimination throughout the century, a burden eased but not ended. Always the last hired and first fired in an economic contraction, it is not difficult to understand why blacks are always so receptive to ideas for economic growth, but always suspicious about any politician who would tamper with the safety net. With periods of economic distress far exceeding periods of real expansion in the last dozen years, it is no wonder blacks are so protective of the safety net. Their discouragement must be profound. Political liberals offer them a safety net and no growth, while political conservatives promise growth but without a safety net. Early in 1978, Senator Orrin G. Hatch of Utah, a fellow Republican and good friend, wrote about one aspect of this problem:

> This is a new slavery worse than the old. I cannot imagine a worse humiliation than to be freed, given civil rights, and then told: "Don't worry, the government will look after you." Leaders in the black community have realized that blacks have been placed in a new position of dependency. The black community gets income transfers, but not opportunities for blacks to earn their own way and to be economically and politically independent. It is not easy to get out of this position.

It will not be easy—nothing worthwhile ever is—but there is only one realistic strategy to get blacks out of this position, a strategy that offers growth without destruction of the safety net.

I have opposed a constitutional amendment which would mandate a balanced federal budget, because such a decree does not address the economic causes of budget deficits. Attempting to balance the budget by raising tax rates, for example, would further slow down growth and increase demand for still more spending. Slashing the safety net, if it succeeded, might do away with the numerical problem, but not the human one. There are even ways to balance the budget—like juggling the federal books with "off-budget budgets," or shifting the burden of repaying our debts to future generations—which either ignore the situation or leave it worse than before. I believe that calls for a constitutional amendment to balance the budget are sincere appeals for the solution to our problems which Congress has failed to provide. But Congress does not fulfill its responsibility for finding solutions simply by writing that appeal into the Constitution.

Because I do not advocate ripping away the safety net of government support services, I am sometimes accused of not wanting to reduce excessive government expenditures. The accusation is misplaced, I think, because the issues are quite separate. Few politicians can be optimistic about the efficiency of federal spending, particularly when the General Accounting Office estimates that up to $25 billion a year is lost to fraud. Still, the whole debate between tax incentives and spending restraints is essentially a matter of emphasis and priorities. What comes first?

Yes, everyone agrees spending restraint is desirable. I take a back seat to no one in this department. But significant spending reductions require both a strong economy and some fundamental long-term plans in order to sustain the required public support. Still it isn't difficult to find some money in a $532 billion dollar budget that could be better spent in reducing taxes and federal borrowing.

Since the Carter administration had already substantially fattened the 1978 and 1979 budgets, a better perspective on the 1980 proposals is gained by comparing them with actual spending in fiscal 1977. That also shows where spending should slow down. The Defense Department's budget will indeed rise a bit more than inflation over those three years—by 28 percent in nominal terms. But the Department of Housing and Urban Development, whose programs are consistently misguided and scandalous, has been rewarded with an 82 percent rise in its budget. Health, Education and Welfare, which admits to losing around $7 billion a year to waste and fraud, captured a 35 percent increase and will now be doling out just a shade under $200 billion.

A look at the 1977–80 increase by function conveys the same impression. Defense up 29 percent. Education, training, employment and social services up 44 percent. Health spending is up 38 percent, and would be higher except for the unbelievable assumption that price controls can disguise the inflationary effect of pouring federal money into this sector. International affairs, mostly foreign aid, is up 71 percent. Energy is up 89 percent. Interest on the national debt is up 90 percent to a staggering $57 billion—over 10 percent of the budget and over 2 cents out of every dollar spent in the whole economy (and that is assuming an unlikely sharp decline in interest rates).

Several long-term trends in federal spending are particularly disturbing, and merit closer, more honest attention than they usually receive. For one thing, while there has been an enormous rise in non-defense spending over the past two decades, there has been as well continual erosion of the share of the budget devoted to defense—from 58 percent in 1955 to 24 percent today. (If defense had held its share of the budget, and social spending grew as it did, then total federal spending would now be almost twice as large as it is.) To cut defense spending from half to a fourth of the budget is obviously a lot easier than cutting it from a fourth to zero. So, the share of total federal spending going to defense cannot possibly decline as rapidly as it has in the past decade or two; indeed it cannot safely decline at all. Nobody seriously argues that future increases in federal non-defense spending can still be financed, year after year, by diverting funds from defense. Either the future growth of social spending must be much slower than in the past, or taxes must extract a steadily larger share of income, or the budget deficit must grow more or less continually over time. That is the uncomfortable reality of the arithmetic.

A second long-term budget problem concerns the aging of our population, and the risky practice of financing Social Security (and some sixty-four other federal pensions) from current taxes. In 1940, 7 percent of the population was over age sixty-five; that figure is now 11 percent and will rise to 18 percent by 2030. While there are currently six active workers for each retired person, there will be no more than three workers per retired person in fifty years. Benefits to the aged currently amount to 24 percent of the federal budget, and are conservatively estimated to rise to 40 percent of the budget by 2025. As of September 1977, the government's unfunded liabilities for annuity programs was $5.4 trillion—that being the promises to pay future pensions from revenues the government does not have. Future pension obligations are a hidden part of our national debt—an enormous claim on future taxpayers—and to honor those debts we must generate sufficient growth so the tax burden does not become overwhelming. These problems could be severely magnified by tax and pension incentives that encourage early retirement, and by the equally strong incentives for the young to go on the dole or into the underground activities in order to avoid sharing so much of their earnings.

A third potential long-term problem involves the increasingly surreptitious use of off-budget agencies to divide up credit and resources toward politically favored uses. This adds more than $12 billion to the real deficit for fiscal 1979, and contributes to the growing possibility of defaults on some of the $224 billion in outstanding federally guaranteed loans. Federal and federally assisted borrowing absorbed a third of all funds raised in credit markets in 1975–1977, making it that much harder for those of us without subsidized or guaranteed loans to raise money for housing construction, mortgages, or business investment.

Any serious effort to limit the growth of spending must deal directly with the areas where most spending growth has occurred. This means, above all, transfer payments to individuals, which have soared from 24 percent of the budget in 1965 to 40 percent today. Economic growth is the obvious antidote for excessive outlays on welfare, disability, and unemployment benefits. The problem today is that if welfare recipients take a job, their benefits (including Medicaid, food stamps and housing allowances) are stripped away, they face commuting and other work-related expenses, and federal and state governments impose hefty income and payroll taxes on their earnings. The net effect, documented in numerous studies, is that the family is often worse off if its head accepts an entry-level job—that is, the marginal tax rate on added earnings exceeds 100 percent. The only solution is to either reduce the benefits from not working—which would be unduly harsh on the needy—or to increase the after-tax rewards for working. Again, the positive approach of income incentives and growth has the effect of reducing the welfare rolls and federal spending without lowering the safety net.

Social Security is in trouble and must be saved. It is perfectly legitimate for a democratic society to require that people set aside something to provide for their old age, their survivors, or unexpected hardship. One way to help make Social Security solvent is not to force people into early retirement, extended unemployment, and permanent "disability" with onerous taxes on work. Another way is to ensure a growing, prosperous economy so that there are enough present workers to finance Social Security without hardship. Third, for the benefit of those now working—the retired of the 1980s, 1990s, and beyond—we must be far more generous about letting people defer taxation on savings put away for retirement. After all, those savings then go into more and better tools to increase future production. In this way, retirement benefits are provided out of the economy's added potential rather than out of taxes levied on future workers.

For similar reasons, and also to motivate older managers and professionals to continue producing, we should provide more generous exemptions from estate taxes and thus encourage people to accumulate shares in a growing economy for their own futures and those of their heirs. In this regard, the additional penalty of sharply reduced Social Security benefits for those who earn more than $4500 after age sixty-five is an especially vicious marginal tax rate that both forces retirement on those who wish to continue working and ensures that retirement income remains inadequate.

Finally, a matter not often enough mentioned in regard to the elderly and their financial security: A healthy stock market is particularly essential to the strength of private pension funds. To an ever-increasing extent, policies that damage stockholders must be viewed as an open assault on pensioners. By whittling away at the investments of pension funds, with taxes and regulations that form a wedge between before-tax business earnings and after-tax stockholder returns, we have been pauperizing pensioners. A growth-oriented tax policy would provide the resources for prosperity for both the retired and working people of the future; absence of such a policy will impoverish both.

Another area of major spending growth is grants to state and local governments, which have grown from about 9 percent of the budget in 1965 to over 16 percent today. The illusion that federal money is free has fostered its misuse, and tied states and cities into a web of restrictions based on the threat of withheld federal aid.

The federal government, though, has no significant source of revenues except the residents of cities and states. When the federal government borrows or taxes more, there is that much less credit on taxable income available for state and local governments. I have supported "revenue sharing" as a short-term emergency measure, because of all federal grants, it involves the least bureaucracy. But in the long run, reduced federal taxation is the purest form of aid to the cities and states—it directly increases their tax base. Other grants or revenue sharing simply take money from the cities and states, subtract a brokerage fee for the federal middlemen, and send part of it back with strings attached.

The apparent alternative of financing grants by printing more money just fuels more inflation, and the inflation causes more problems for states and cities than the grants can solve. Converting local deficits into federal deficits in this way, through a policy that might be called "deficit sharing," is a dangerous practice that helped push Italy toward the brink of financial ruin.

Rather than simply taking a smaller share of the nation's income, the federal government chooses to raise taxes and return a portion in the form of grants or revenue sharing. A total of 534 federal grant programs to state and local governments now generate over 49 million transactions with federal agencies each year—a paperwork burden that costs state and local governments some $5 billion annually.

The strings on federal "aid" can be terribly binding. Many grants are linked to "tax effort," which means that more money flows to communities that tax the stuffing out of their residents. If they cut taxes to attract and retain productive enterprises and individuals, cities and states actually lose federal aid. Some $16 billion in grants is tied to notoriously crude estimates of local unemployment, giving local officials a perverse incentive to perpetuate destructive tax and regulatory policies. Or the grants may be based on a state's before-tax income per person, which neglects the vast differences between states in taxes and other living costs. A dollar of income goes a lot further in the rural South than in the urban Northeast, so that per capita income before taxes is a poor measure of respective needs or of the ability to bear more taxes.

Since there are no truly objective criteria for deciding who should get what from federal spending, the actual outcome tends to reflect political clout. But somehow, despite the fact that the Northeast and North Central regions lost eight seats in the House of Representatives as a result of population losses detected by the 1970 census, the Democratic politicians of the Northeast—especially those in New York and New Jersey—promise to jiggle the grant formulas to benefit their older industrial areas. They can hardly be more successful now, with fewer representatives, than they have been in the past. National economic growth is the only answer.

My constituents around Buffalo, among the most heavily taxed Americans, understand this. In 1968, over 62 percent of all federal grants designed to help cities went to cities with over 500,000 population; by 1975, the large cities' share was down to 44 percent. The revenue-sharing law requires that no local government get more than 145 percent of the average per capita payment to localities in each state, thus preventing a concentration of resources where the need is greatest. Public make-work schemes, under the Comprehensive Employment and Training

Act, have increasingly been spread among newer cities and suburbs, with older big cities receiving only 22 percent of the funds.

It is ironic that some people see the salvation of New York City or Buffalo in ever larger federal grants and loans. Actually, the cities have long been treated as a natural resource that could be tapped continually without becoming depleted. The federal government imposed steep taxes on city businesses and residents first in order to finance westward expansion, then rural modernization, and then suburbanization. Federal policies invariably stressed new construction rather than the maintenance and renewal of the existing stocks of social capital—housing, highways, railroads, and utilities—that were located predominantly in the older cities. Federal highway and mass transit programs provided arteries to draw people out of the cities, with little of the cost being borne by suburban commuters. Housing programs concentrated their efforts on new towns and new suburban housing tracts. The Tennessee Valley Authority and Rural Electrification Administration provided subsidized energy to develop rural areas. There were costly schemes to create "model cities" and "new communities," drawing resources away from the older cities.

As the federal government moved into more and more areas of responsibility, it pre-empted a larger share of the available tax base. As recently as 1936, local governments alone (not even counting state governments) raised more revenue than the federal government. Now, when people are finished paying their federal taxes, there is precious little left to finance their own communities' basic social services—police and fire protection, streets and schools—

which are still overwhelmingly a local responsibility. By running large and chronic budget deficits, the federal government also borrows a huge portion of available savings, making it harder for state and local governments to raise funds for essential capital improvements.

A major cost of that increasing centralization is not financial, but the loss of flexibility, variety, and innovation in local government. The federal government is rarely an innovator in public services. Its huge and monolithic bureaucracy forces a dull conformity on the diverse wants of our many unique communities. This is a big country, with plenty of room for different tastes in public services and different ways of accomplishing common objectives.

Local tastes and varieties, though, are annoying to those who plan from the top, because it is inconvenient to accommodate them in uniform schemes. But the country's enormous diversity is a source of great strength, expanding the range of choice available to people, fostering new ways of doing things, and allowing us to learn from one another. Competition in local government services accomplishes the same result as competition in private services—it fosters the highest quality at the lowest possible cost.

Government does not like competition, any more than a private business or a labor union enjoys competition. This is because it must pay for its errors. When the government of New York spends tax dollars inefficiently relative to the government of Connecticut, it must watch in dismay as a number of its citizens and businesses leave New York for Connecticut. The citizens left behind in New York to pay the bills will, if they can, try to get the federal government to tax the rest of the nation to help them pay the bills. When the federal government lays new taxes on the nation, the nation loses competitiveness relative to the rest of the world; and people, capital, and businesses relocate abroad. Political pressures then develop to halt this exodus, i.e., capital controls, taxes on U.S. multinational corporations, tariffs and quotas on foreign imports. If the process continues, it can only end in the total control and impoverishment of the nation.

Having made these observations, I must add that I am not optimistic about the chances for decentralization of federal programs, at least for a number of years. As inefficient as it is, this is after all the federal safety net we're talking about. Unraveling this amalgam of programs— slashing federal welfare, housing, education, food, transportation programs—leaves us back where we started, with New York and other states bleeding to death because a diminishing number of citizens and enterprises must finance public debt created by earlier governments. (It is easy enough to say that a segment of the nation must pay for its own sins, excesses, and errors; but there always comes a point where the rest of the nation—responding the way a family would—relents and helps the wayward brother.) Moreover, especially in the Northeast, where the citizenry has experienced years of economic decline, there is a natural suspicion of eliminating what is perceived to be our national insurance, our pooling of risk. In the 1980s, after a stretch of real economic growth in the Northeast, such suspicions might be sufficiently dampened to begin trading off less central control for more local flexibility.

At the outset, though, there is no substitute for productive private jobs. Many of the problems of New York City are, in reality, symptoms of a shortage of jobs. Housing deteriorates, for example, because incomes (and therefore rents) are insufficient to justify housing maintenance. Crime is partly linked to idleness, low income, and the frustration of human potential by the "system." City budget problems often reflect the squeeze of rising welfare expenses and falling taxable incomes—both symptoms of inadequate job opportunities, and of artificial barriers to such opportunities that would otherwise exist.

The public sector can help by providing a tax and regulatory climate that is more favorable to business creation and expansion in the cities—a climate that eases investors' fears and somewhat smooths the federal, state, and local regulatory obstacle course. It also requires efforts to ease the tax burden on income from job-creating investments. Here, simply easing the burden on new investments alone is not enough: it could easily result in a correspondingly heavier load for older, perhaps weaker industries.

At the local level, to the extent allowed by federal regulation, there must be a concerted effort to lessen any barriers to economic advancement. Building codes and zoning laws are often unduly restrictive; occupational licensing and paternalistic labor laws often deny work to those unable to penetrate their barriers. As an example, consider that a license to operate a taxi in New York City now trades for over $50,000, and this formidable investment keeps many out of the taxi business, keeps cab fares artificially high, and thereby promotes excessive use of private automobiles. In addition, property taxes could profitably be revised to fall more heavily on land, rather than, as at present, penalizing property improvements.

New Hampshire provides a provocative example that the problems of other Northern states are not simply a matter of climate or location. With no sales or personal income tax, no state plans limiting development, New Hampshire has attracted more than 220 new plants or corporate headquarters in five years, bringing over 14,-000 jobs to the state. A study by Colin and Rita Campbell of Dartmouth suggests that New Hampshire's public services are not inferior to those of the high-tax, depressed economy of nearby Vermont. In any case, the demand for public services, like the demand for anything else, depends on the price. The fact that New Hampshire's population soared 15 percent since 1970, far more than even California's, indicates that many people consider the balance of taxes and services about right. Others can learn from such regional experiments, yet I would not favor imposing the New Hampshire model on areas with different desires. As with any plan of purposeful decentralization of public services, politicians need a better reading of the true nature of the public's demand for tax-financed services at various levels of government.

One proposal that clearly moves in an opposite direction is a compulsory national monopoly on health insurance. Instead of increased emphasis on private, competitive services, or on levels of government closer to those involved, a nationalized health plan would move to the opposite extreme. Federal spending would rise an estimated $120 billion a year to begin with, and such estimates have proved optimistic in the past.

The idea of health insurance—pooling our risks to to guard against the unforeseen—is a sound one. But the United Kingdom experience, with its poor quality and widespread shortages of care, shows that nationalization is not the most humane method. I believe the federal government should provide some sort of coverage for catastrophic illnesses, maintain adequate health services for the poor and the old, and concentrate on encouraging private health insurers to expand their regular coverage, which now touches nearly 90 percent of the people. Citizens should be overwhelmed neither by the costs of a long and expensive illness nor by the burden of an inefficient nationalized health system.

The federal government already spends more than $50 billion on health. That spending has surely pushed up the cost of medical services, and enriched providers of these services almost as much as it has helped the sick. About one-fourth of Medicaid money is apparently lost to fraud, for example, and new scandals continually pop up in the news. Nationalized health insurance sounds a lot like more of the same. The notion that the federal government can effectively control medical costs, much less the quality of care, leads me to wonder whether I wouldn't prefer some alternative to being delivered in an ambulance as reliable as AMTRAK to a hospital operated like the Postal Service!

Whatever one's views of particular programs, however, one thing is certain. A prosperous private economy can easily afford a strong safety net of public services. A stifled, smothering economy can't. A prosperous economy can afford to care for our elderly, police our neighborhoods, school our children, and pave our roads. Private affluence does not mean public squalor.

6 *Ending Inflation, Now*

In 1978, President Carter's Treasury Secretary, Michael Blumenthal, explained that "inflation is caused by a number of factors that act together and interact in strange and mysterious ways." President Carter has suggested that inflation is caused by "attitudes and habits." Other officials explain inflation by a circular definition—that inflation is "caused" by rising prices or costs. There is even the excuse that we are simply at the mercy of the gods: "To get a significant improvement in the inflation rate," says Professor Lester Thurow of the Massachusetts Institute of Technology, "the U.S. needs some good luck."

None of this is helpful or hopeful. There is nothing strange and mysterious about inflation. It is not visited upon us by nature. Inflation is not caused by labor unions demanding higher wages, and it is not caused by business marking up the price of its goods and services. *Inflation is a decline in the value of the currency produced by the government. The government and the government alone has control over the value of the currency it produces.*

Over thousands of years we have learned that when a government guarantees the value of its currency, by promising to redeem it at any time in the future with something of value in a fixed amount, there is no inflation. Whatever the international monetary system or standard of value—usually silver, gold, or some other precious metal—periods of stable prices have always depended on such a guarantee. If the government indeed acts on its guarantee, there is no decline in the value of its currency, no inflation.

For more than two hundred years in Great Britain, from 1717 to 1931, there was absolutely no inflation. The general price level remained constant, except for minor variations, because the government kept its promise during that long span to redeem its currency with a fixed amount of something of value, in this case, gold. Throughout the history of the United States, until 1933, there was no inflation except during brief periods of wartime when the promise to redeem the dollar into gold was suspended. The dollar began its decline in value in 1933 when President Roosevelt reduced the amount of gold that the dollar could buy. That is, with the dollar having less value in terms of something real and palpable, individuals were forced to demand more of them in exchange for their labor, and businessmen were forced to ask more of them in the prices of their goods. Inflation!

If it is basically as simple as this, why don't we do it? Why doesn't the U.S. government once again guarantee the value of the dollars it produces by promising to redeem them with something of value? In fact, why did the government ever stop this practice, proven and time-tested over the centuries?

It started with the mistaken theory, back in the 1930s, that government could make up for its tax and regulatory mistakes with "stimulative" (that is, inflationary) money policy. Instead of changing the tax and tariff laws which pitched us into the Great Depression, the new theory said that creating surplus dollars would "stimulate demand"— fool people into believing that the additional paper in circulation really was an increase in the nation's wealth. Ever since, to some degree, our fiscal and monetary policies have been backwards. Our tax rates and regulations have been a drag on the economy instead of providing incentives for economic growth, and our monetary policy has attempted without success to compensate, causing inflation instead of preventing it.

After a while it became clear that excessively inflating the money supply only causes inflation and worsens stagnation. But during times of economic distress, many people benefit from inflation or at least think they do, and political pressures build up that tempt the government to continue the inflation. The individuals who benefit are those who borrowed money in good times, expecting good times would continue and they would be able to pay off their debt. But with hard times they must work much harder to pay off that debt. Because the debt is reckoned in dollars, if the government reduces the value of the dollars, wages and prices are forced to rise and the individual can pay off the debt with less effort. The problem is that the individual who lent the money in good times, the creditor, expected that the dollars paid back would be of equal value, and they are not. If the society wants to assist debtors, this is all well and good, but the process is not one that can be repeated without poisoning the whole system. Individuals who want to save and invest, the creditors, cannot be repeatedly discouraged by the shrinking of the value of the money owed them, or they will be discouraged from saving and investing. With the addition of progressivity in income taxes, the problem is compounded, for as the value of the dollar declines and the general price level rises, individuals who want to save and invest find it increasingly harder to earn the money to do so. Now in higher tax brackets, and doing exactly the same amount of work, the rewards after taxes from their production are reduced.

The reason a monetary standard works so well is because it is democratic. This may sound like a strange way of putting it, *but when the government agrees to maintain the value of the currency it produces, the people are in control of the money supply.* When the government prints one dollar more than the citizens need for the purposes of trading the goods and services they produce, one citizen will come to the government with that dollar and ask to redeem it, and the government gives up the promised weight in gold. When this happens, the government is alerted that it has been excessive in its money creation.

On the other hand, when the government produces one dollar less than is needed for these transaction purposes, someone will come to the government with the appropriate weight in gold and ask for a dollar. This alerts the government that it is printing an insufficient supply of dollars. The monetary standard thus serves as an error signal, with the people of the country at the switch, as long as the government maintains its guarantee.

If government refuses to abide by its guarantee, it loses

the efficiency of this error signal. Government must then find a way to conduct monetary policy wisely, in a way that maintains the value of its currency without the use of gold or some other commodity of value. This is the condition that prevails today in the United States, with the Federal Reserve in charge of trying to find that wise policy.

In this environment, inflation arises to the extent that the supply of money grows faster than people in the United States, or outside the U.S. for that matter, demand dollars for transaction purposes. We often hear the phrase that inflation is always a matter of "too much money chasing too few goods." This idea at least begins to explain the problem faced by the monetary authority. Once this simple idea is grasped, it's clear that inflation can only be eliminated by printing less money and producing more goods.

The public, though, is often told that curing inflation requires higher taxes, higher unemployment, slower economic growth, and a ceiling on pay increases. These "cures" follow from the idea that individuals cause inflation through their wage and price greed, and that the government has no hand in the decline of the value of its currency. But inflation is not caused by workers working, business doing business, consumers consuming, or producers producing. Wages, prices, and profits no more cause inflation than wet streets cause rain. Little wonder that these kinds of cures for inflation are both unpopular and ineffective. In the hot summer of 1968, when the American public was about to be socked with a 10 percent tax surcharge, Professor Walter Heller argued that the tax hike was "a vital step toward economic stability." The economy soon slipped into a deep recession while inflation, still fueled by sloppy monetary policy, continued unchecked.

The notion that a tax increase could have eased the rising cost of living was a contradiction in terms. Taxes are themselves the fastest-rising part of the cost of living. While the cost of maintaining an intermediate family budget rose 88 percent from 1967 to 1977, that family's personal income and payroll taxes rose 211 percent.

A similar confusion is involved in the idea that we can lower living costs by switching from one tax to another—lowering taxes that are directly counted in most indexes that measure inflation (sales taxes) while raising taxes that are not so counted (income taxes). In October 1978, for example, President Carter opposed "any further reduction in federal income taxes" while simultaneously supporting "tax cuts which could directly lower costs and prices." Yet taxes are part of the cost of living—the price of public services. The fact that conventional measures of the general price level do not include all taxes does not change reality.

Those who have convinced themselves that higher taxes are a cure for inflation naturally view our tax-rate reduction proposals as inflationary. Yet reduced tax rates are inflationary only if they result in larger budget deficits and those larger deficits are financed by creating more money. A constructive reduction of steep marginal tax rates can increase the tax base by increasing the volume of work, saving, and investment, and by reducing the incentive to evade taxes. A growth-oriented tax policy also reduces the clamor for federal spending to support incomes of those unemployed or otherwise needy. Lacy

H. Hunt, senior vice president and chief economist of Fidelity Bank of Philadelphia, last year was at first skeptical of the Kemp-Roth proposal. But after examination of it, he reported to the bank and its customers that the bill "would in fact serve to relieve inflationary pressures now and in future years. Such a proposal would raise productivity and investment and contribute to a stronger dollar."

Neither Andrew Mellon's nor President Kennedy's reductions in excessively high marginal income tax rates increased the budget deficit *for even one year.* And both these cuts in marginal tax rates resulted in enormous increases in private saving during the economic expansion that followed. These historical examples increase our confidence that even if a slightly larger federal budget deficit were to emerge temporarily, the resources of increased state and local revenues and private saving could easily finance the federal deficit without creating a need to print more money. With a tax policy that encourages personal saving, there would be more funds available for both public and private borrowers without either driving interest rates sky high or flooding the system with more money.

A second idea—that slow growth, or even recession, is a cure for inflation—is really difficult to understand. If we agree that inflation is too much money chasing too few goods, it obviously isn't going to help to have fewer goods. Nor is higher unemployment—yet another poisonous "cure" for inflation—consistent with common sense. The idea that more inflation will give us less unemployment, and vice versa, has long been a cornerstone of national economic policy under Republicans as well as Democrats. This concept of the "Phillips Curve," named after a British economist, was imported into this country by Professors Robert Samuelson and Robert Solow in 1960. "In order to achieve the nonperfectionist's goal of ... no more than 3 percent unemployment," wrote Samuelson and Solow, "the price index might have to rise by as much as 4 to 5 percent per year."

When inflation soared above 12 percent in 1974, with unemployment still well above 5 percent, the idea that one could simply trade a little inflation for a low unemployment rate ceased to be respectable outside the White House. Insofar as it ever worked, the Phillips Curve was based on the unwholesome idea of deceiving workers into taking a hidden cut in real income. Prices would supposedly rise faster than wages—cutting real wages, boosting profit margins, and making it profitable to hire more workers. Lord Keynes himself thought this was a nifty idea: "Reductions of real wages arising in this way are not, as a rule, resisted," wrote Keynes, and "no trade union would dream of striking on every occasion of a rise in the cost of living."

Actually, the scheme goes back at least to 1705, when John Law wrote that "an addition to the money will employ the people that are now idle." But workers are not so easily deceived. Even the hint of more inflationary policies today brings swift reaction in the form of higher wage rates, higher interest rates, and a sinking dollar. Markets have become acutely sensitive to monetary excesses, so that policies to pump up spending are quickly dissipated in higher costs.

Although the Carter administration continues to talk as though proposals to reduce inflation are synonymous with proposals to increase unemployment, few people really buy that line any more. Representative Parren Mitchell, a Democrat and chairman of the congressional black caucus, recently delivered the obituary on the Phillips Curve at the University of Wisconsin: "Historically, when inflation is above the 3 percent to 4 percent level, rises in inflation have been accompanied with increases in the aggregate rate of unemployment, and a disproportionate share of that unemployment is relegated to the black community. Black teenage employment, in particular, has been the victim of the Phillips Curve trade-off theory."

Because it has proven impossible to reduce real wages by inflation, and thus foster more employment, the former apostles of the Phillips Curve have been drawn toward explicit controls on wages combined with continued inflation of prices. Barry Bosworth, head of the Council on Wage and Price Stability, has pointed out that this was the effect of Nixon's 5.5 percent wage controls; it was also the effect of Lyndon Johnson's 3.2 percent guideline. We can only assume that reducing real wages is again the intent of President Carter's 7 percent guideline. Adam Smith observed the pattern of two centuries ago: "Whenever the law has attempted to regulate the wages of workmen," he wrote, "it has always been rather to lower them than to raise them."

When word of President Carter's wage guideline proposal reached the markets last October, the assessment of its value was brutally apparent. The stock market dropped 100 points during the planning, announcement, and explanation of the scheme; the dollar continued its plunge on the foreign-exchange markets; and interest rates soared. No wonder. The "anti-inflation" program would only impose new regulations on the transaction economy—reducing its efficiency—without a word about maintaining the value of the dollar by reducing the supply of them. The adverse effect of this plan on the markets was at last so obvious that in November the President took more correct steps, announcing that the U.S. would defend the dollar by buying up surplus quantities of them with foreign-denominated bonds, gold, and borrowed foreign currencies. On announcement of this plan, the market rose 35 points in a single day, bond prices rose, long-term interest rates fell, and the price of gold plummeted from its record high of $243 per ounce.

The idea that holding down workers' real wages can reduce inflation tends to puzzle the factory workers in my Buffalo-area district, who by this definition have been fighting inflation since 1967. That's the last time they had a real raise in real take-home pay. I'm always amazed that the party historically linked with organized labor—the Democrats—should be so anxious to blame inflation on labor and attempt to impose guidelines or controls on wages. Perhaps it is because they believe they can safely take labor's support for granted, regardless of their blatant anti-labor policies. Thus Barry Bosworth goes around saying things like "These major unions have to be brought back into line," and "If government has any part to play in fighting inflation, it must have a role in private wage and price decisions." Democratic economists like Arthur Okun and Walter Heller are particularly fond of a "tax-based incomes policy," which is little more than a tax on pay increases.

Actually, labor unions are just a handy scapegoat for the government's own inflationary policies. A few unions may gain relative advantages for their members (perhaps by limiting job opportunities with restrictive licensing laws), but they do so only by driving other workers into more competitive labor markets, depressing wages there. Similarly, blaming inflation on big business has no basis in logic or evidence, though Federal Reserve Chairman G. William Miller wants to solve inflation by taxing profits. (No matter what the problem is, somebody always wants to solve it with more taxes.) We had big business and big unions before the late 1960s, but there was barely any inflation; and prior to 1933 there was none at all.

The whole idea that political officials should dictate what a person's labor or property is worth, through guidelines or controls, would strike me as morally offensive and politically dangerous, even if it worked to halt inflation. But the fact of the matter is that particular wages and prices have nothing to do with inflation, which is the decline in the value of money. Wages and prices both rise when there are inflationary pressures, but that doesn't prove that wages push prices, or vice versa—only that both labor and product markets are affected by too much money. And if some wages or prices are held down by government decree, it only means that workers and producers have less incentive to work and produce and fewer of the goods they were producing come into the market. If it were possible to control all the millions of prices in an economy (think about used goods, new fashions, commodities priced in world markets), we would only see chronic excess demand for all goods and widespread shortages of all goods. The empty meat counters and drowned chicks of 1974 are typical of a controlled economy. There was little satisfaction then in knowing that if there had been any meat to buy, it would have been a few pennies cheaper. Once controls were lifted, supplies soared and meat prices fell.

One of my favorite stories along these lines is about the woman who complains to the grocer that he charges a dollar for a dozen eggs. "The grocer across town only charges seventy-five cents," she tells him. "Well, lady, why don't you buy your eggs from him?" The lady says, "Well, he is out of eggs." To which the grocer replies, "Oh, when I'm out of eggs I only charge seventy cents a dozen."

Prices have important work to do, in signaling businessmen about what consumers value most highly. If prices and wages are not free to respond to market signals of supply and demand, there will be no incentive for labor and capital to move to the most promising opportunities. The result will be wasted resources, less production, and more inflation.

Since persistent inflation is a matter of too much money bidding for too little production, we need a system that will keep money and output in better balance. A tax and regulatory environment conducive to growth will certainly help. But it isn't enough. The productive, private sector can expand and thereby reduce inflationary pressures, but the government can still make errors in its conduct of monetary policy in ways that reduce the value of the dollar. What is urgently needed is some sort of external discipline, a standard by which to judge whether money is or is not too abundant. Money is too important to be anchored in the shifting sands of political pressures and controlled by a handful of "experts." The American people can best say when too much money is in circulation, and they ought to be given the chance.

In his memoirs, former President Nixon recalled that Arthur Burns had advised against unleashing the dollar from outside constraints. "This was to be one of the few cases in which I did not follow his recommendations. I decided to close the gold window and let the dollar float. As events unfolded, this decision turned out to be the best thing that came out of the economic program I announced on August 15, 1971."

Looking back on that decision I have come to believe that closing the gold window (which had been inching shut for several years) was a crucial error—eliminating the only surviving limit on monetary expansion, undermining the confidence in the dollar, and permitting the runaway explosion of the U.S. money supply that helped spread the infection of inflation throughout the world in 1972–73 and ever since.

Contrary to President Nixon's belief, as also stated in his book, the 1944 Bretton Woods agreements did not require the United States to fix exchange rates between the dollar and other currencies. All that was required was that the dollar be tied at a fixed price (thirty-five dollars an ounce) to gold. Because the dollar was "as good as gold," it became the pivot of the international monetary system, the unit in which oil and many other globally traded goods were priced. The dollar became the major "reserve currency" for the world, as other nations voluntarily tied themselves to the U.S. dollar and their governments were content to accumulate the currency of this most secure, powerful, and responsible nation as a reserve of buying power.

As central banker to the world, the United States did not have to be concerned, as others did, about running out of foreign currency reserves when imports exceeded exports, or when dollar investments abroad exceeded foreign dollars invested here. Dollars were accepted everywhere, after all, and we could never run out of dollars because we could always create more. The catch, of course, is that by abusing this privilege—by not living up to our responsibilities—the dollar became less and less acceptable in world commerce. The value of the dollar began its decline.

In the late 1960s, the constructive tax and trade policies initiated by President Kennedy and his Treasury Secretary Douglas Dillon early in the decade began to be undermined by steadily increasing rates of money creation. Growth of the money supply accelerated steadily from an austere 1 percent a year from 1959 to 1961 to almost 5 percent by 1966. The flood of dollars spilled over into our balance of payments, as more dollars were spent and invested abroad than found their way back here. Foreign central banks found themselves piling up vast hoards of unwanted dollars, which they then invested in U.S. government securities. Foreign exporters, holding more dollars than they wanted to spend or invest here, traded them for, say, German marks or Japanese yen. The German and Japanese central banks bought the dollars by printing more of their own currencies, thus importing our inflation.

Growing weary of this situation, some foreign central banks demanded U.S. gold for the surplus dollars they held. The policy of Presidents Johnson and Nixon had been to prevent such a move, and with some arm-twisting they had succeeded up to that time. But with the threat of a massive outflow of U.S. gold reserves, we were forced either to stop supplying more dollars than people were willing to hold or to renege on our promise to redeem dollars for gold at the agreed price. Unfortunately, we chose to eliminate the discipline of gold. The purchasing power of the dollar—its value—has been sinking ever since, both at home and abroad.

In 1977 and 1978, foreign central banks were again forced to mop up tens of billions of excess dollars sloshing around in foreign markets. This time, however, they tired quickly of playing a game rigged against them, and began working on a bold plan to create a European currency unit to reduce the central role of the dollar as a reserve currency. Led by the Germans and French, the new European monetary system would aim to insulate European nations against the U.S. inflation and provide a zone of monetary stability in Europe. They were wise enough to put something of value—gold—at the heart of the system.

Without U.S. support, the plan is not likely to succeed in its announced objective. Europe is too fragmented and militarily vulnerable to provide the stability essential to a world trading currency. Still, the sheer desperation of the move serves as a stern warning to us. The plunge of the dollar in 1978 was no doubt related to the increasing attractiveness of the new resolve in Europe to provide monetary stability. International transactors shifted their dollar bank accounts into marks, francs, and yen. President Carter, who had been advised that an austere energy bill would stop the decline of the dollar (it didn't) and that a stiff wage-price control scheme would do the same (it didn't), finally began to take some correct measures in November 1978, when he announced his plan of direct dollar support by monetary means.

In the 1980s, we cannot continue to have these currency convulsions if we are to achieve sustained prosperity. The great global prosperity of the late 1960s was closely tied to the improved environment for international trade and investment; the growth of world trade far outpaced the growth of domestic economies. But wild swings in currency values, especially that of the dollar—the world trading currency—reduced the efficiency of international trade by discouraging international traders. In order to repeat the sustained global rise in living standards of the 1960s, it will be necessary to provide a monetary unit of sufficiently predictable value to be generally accepted throughout the world. The world desperately needs a secure anchor, a standard of value by which to measure things and in which to make long-term plans and contracts.

The U.S. dollar is uniquely suited to this crucial function of being the world's central reserve and trading currency. All that is required is a firm commitment to tie the dollar's value to something more constant than political whim. We must restore a monetary standard. In theory, almost any commodity or even a basket of goods would do. In practice, such a measuring rod must be convenient to handle and not subject to wild fluctuations, since a government needs to keep an inventory on hand to use as a monetary error signal. Gold has been chosen historically, not out of any mystique or fetish, but because of its generally accepted exchange value, limited supply, compactness, and imperishability.

By offering to redeem dollars for gold at some fixed price, the dollar would instantly regain its position as the linchpin of world commerce. Even if the gold window were open only to foreign central banks but not to U.S. citizens, that would be an important step forward. As in the post-1933 period, people at home or abroad who distrusted dollars could trade them for other currencies; foreign central banks would act as their agent by redeeming surplus dollars for gold. Any such outflow of gold would have to be taken as a signal that the supply of dollars exceeded the demand, requiring corrective action by the monetary authorities. Once we recognize the silliness of keeping the gold window closed to U.S. citizens while keeping it open to representatives of foreign citizens, we would return to the pre-1933 period and the experience of several centuries without inflation.

The hoard of gold at Fort Knox—about 9,000 tons—right now serves no monetary purpose. The Treasury has been auctioning it off in dribbles. Yet there is no reason why we shouldn't auction off some of this inventory to the private market, keeping prudent stocks of a few thousand tons in order to reinstitute dollar convertibility. You don't need great gold tonnage to run a monetary standard. All you need is that error signal. Britain successfully operated its monetary standard for centuries with only a tiny gold reserve. Nor do we need to have a great deal of gold in back of every dollar in circulation, only enough to give the government time to adjust the dollar supply when the error signal flashes its warning. There would be no more inflation as we have known it.

With the dollar once again linked to gold, foreign dollar holders would lose the apprehensions that have led them to substitute other currencies for dollars in their reserves, thus hastening the dollar's decline in value. Long-term expectations of inflation would disappear virtually overnight (as long as we knew the government was serious), and the expected inflation built into nominal interest rates would likewise disappear. If you knew your $100 would be redeemed by the government ten, twenty or thirty years from now with an ounce of gold, you would quickly sense there could be no general price inflation. *If one commodity (money) is fixed to gold—or to any other commodity, the dollar value of all other commodities is more or less fixed.* Try to imagine, for example, inflation carrying a loaf of bread to $100 when the same $100 will buy an ounce of gold. A pound of apples will not go to $100 and a pound of oranges remain at $1. Consumers will shift out of apples into oranges, and orange producers will shift into apple production until price equivalencies are restored.

With a restoration of dollar convertibility into some commodity of value, inflation would not be just a little less virulent, but would be stopped dead in its tracks, as long as we continued to adhere to the monetary standard. We could look forward to long-term interest rates, on mortgages and the like, of around 3 percent, with even lower short-term rates. If this sounds Utopian, that's only because we have forgotten what a monetary standard is all about.

"The commerce and industry of the country," wrote Adam Smith, "cannot be altogether so secure when they are thus, as it were, suspended upon the Daedalian wings of paper money as when they travel upon the solid ground of gold. . . ."

These ideas, I think, provide only a framework for a strategy to end inflation. It would be unrealistic, after all, to suggest that a restoration of dollar convertibility could occur overnight. We have lived with inflation for so long, and so many contracts have been drawn with inflation assumed, that monetary reforms must be carefully planned in order to minimize dislocations that an end of inflation would bring. Nor can the United States do these things in isolation, or dictate international monetary policy to the rest of the world. And any new international monetary agreement must improve upon the weaknesses which led to the breakup of the Bretton Woods system. But serious efforts to reconstruct a stable international monetary system—beginning with a worldwide conference of all our trading partners—must be a central part of our strategy. The sooner such discussions can begin, the sooner we can rid our economic system of the poison of inflation.

7 *Plenty of Energy*

By now, you will not be surprised that the official cure for our energy problems, like the supposed cure for inflation, always involves more taxes. In the Carter administration's first energy proposal of early 1977, there was to be a crude-oil tax, a standby tax on gasoline, a "gas guzzler" tax on cars, and a highly selective tax on certain industries that use natural gas or oil. The American people opposed the taxes and they fell, one by one in Congress. In 1979, the President was back with a new energy package, again determined to solve the problem with taxes, sweeping "windfall" profits taxes on energy producers.

The idea, apparently, is that because a foreign oil cartel (OPEC) had made energy uncomfortably scarce and expensive, the solution was to make energy even more scarce and expensive. In addition to higher energy prices, the U.S. economy should also be blessed with higher energy taxes, amounting to tens of billions of dollars each year—or so the administration's reasoning seems to have gone.

Taxpayers were also saddled with the cost of an enormous new bureaucracy, the Department of Energy—the $11 billion budget which is larger than the cost of our oil imports from Saudi Arabia, larger than the profits of the biggest seven companies, larger than the annual value of all the oil produced in Texas, and about equal to the value of all natural gas produced in this country.

When it comes to energy policy, the Carter administration has waged the "moral equivalent of war" on the American people—and most of all upon our own domestic energy producers. Together, the administration's taxes and regulations are driving an enormous wedge between the prices consumers pay for energy and the prices domestic producers receive, thus causing shortages. American people face the worst possible alternatives—higher energy prices, higher taxes, and lower energy supplies.

Although real after-tax wages have been virtually stagnant for a decade, and real profits adjusted for inflation have fallen, there is talk of even more "sacrifice" and "austerity." Energy is to be saved for some distant rainy day, *but the rainy day is already here!*

The excuse for this dismal regimen of belt-tightening has been, of course, the prediction that the world is about to run out of oil and natural gas. As energy czar James Schlesinger put it: "By the middle 1980s we shall have to face a practical limit worldwide on oil production."

The history of energy abounds with such doomsday forecasts. There was great concern in fifteenth-century Britain that the island would soon run out of firewood, yet Robin Hood's forests are still intact. Early in the nineteenth century, anxiety turned to the imminent depletion of whale oil in America. The real price of high-quality whale oil quadrupled from 1823 to 1855, making it economically attractive to replace whale oil with gas and kerosene made from coal and, later, with refined petroleum.

The U.S. Geological Survey has predicted the imminent exhaustion of U.S. oil almost on a regular basis—in 1914, 1926, 1939, and 1949. In 1936, for example, official data showed that if we continued to use petroleum at even the depressed 1933 rate, the country would run out of "proved reserves" in fifteen years. Yet U.S. proved reserves of petroleum kept rising—from 7 billion in 1920 to 19 billion in 1940 to around 30 billion in early 1978. Worldwide known oil reserves likewise soared from 276 billion in 1958 to at least 646 billion in 1978.

On April 20, 1977, President Carter addressed Congress: "If it were possible for world demand to continue rising during the 1980s at the present rate of 5 percent a year," said the President, "we could use up all the proven reserves of oil in the entire world by the end of the next decade." In a similar televised address almost exactly two years later, in April 1979, he said nothing had happened in the meantime to make him change his mind. *The trouble with that statement is that it has almost always been equally true in the past. Proved reserves have rarely exceeded ten to twenty years' supply because there is no reason to drill, develop, and thus "prove" greater inventories than that.* And coal reserves have always looked vastly greater than oil and gas reserves, because methods of proving coal reserves are less rigorous and costly.

Proved reserves are simply an estimate of what can be recovered from known reservoirs with given technology at present prices. Increase exploration, improve the technology, or raise the price, and proved reserves instantly become much larger. The best estimates of ultimately recoverable reserves have, like those for proved reserves, shown a clear tendency to grow larger with experience— from 600 billion barrels in 1942, to two trillion in 1970, to four trillion by 1973.

By no coincidence, the Central Intelligence Agency launched a seven-page "study" a few days before the administration announced its initial energy tax scheme. The agency's ambiguous conclusion was that "by 1982 or 1983, sizable price increases are inevitable unless large-scale conservation measures cut demand sharply." The CIA suddenly became a marvelously objective source, widely quoted—indeed, misquoted—by those who stood to benefit from the President's curious combination of taxes and subsidies.

Unfortunately, the ink was barely dry on the CIA "study" before its findings were obsolete. New oil and natural gas started popping up unexpectedly all over the place—in Mexico, Canada, China, the North Sea, Alaska. The turmoil in Iran in early 1979 caused some unexpected temporary problems, although half of the estimated U.S. shortfall was initially due to pouring 300,000 barrels a day into a reserve that could not be emptied. The CIA's crucial assumption that the Soviet Union—the world's largest oil producer—would soon be importing oil was ridiculed by all outside experts. The CIA study somehow assumed as well that the soaring price of oil would *decrease* conservation and *increase* the use of oil in place of other fuels—strange behavior indeed.

In the ensuing "battle of the studies," other doomsday and no-growth reports have not fared any better than the

CIA's. A remarkably superficial volume, *A Time to Choose*, published at great expense by the Ford Foundation, was thoroughly discredited by Louis Lapham, the editor of *Harper's*. The Club of Rome, whose computer exercises once predicted exhaustion of everything, did an about-face in a sequel. And a group of not-so-disinterested OPEC and U.S. energy industry representatives put out a book under Massachusetts Institute of Technology auspices which managed to predict shortages with barely a mention of supply, demand, or price.

Meanwhile, two genuine energy experts at MIT, Professors Robert Hall and Robert Pindyck, were getting far less publicity with their conclusion in *The Public Interest* that price controls on oil and gas have pushed demand 8 percent higher and supply 6 percent lower than they were, adding 5 million barrels a day to U.S. imports. Similarly, an early report for the Commission on Critical Choices by the distinguished physicist Dr. Edward Teller received scant attention. Dr. Teller figured that, with a little effort, by 1985 the U.S. could be producing 6 million more barrels of oil a day, and 5.5 trillion more cubic feet of natural gas.

Harder for the press to ignore was the United Nations' report on a gathering of world energy experts in Austria in 1976. In the UN report, Dr. Joseph Barnea pointed out that *the U.S. Geological survey's definition of crude oil simply excludes about 99 percent of what is potentially available*—oil that can be brought up under pressure, tar sands, oil shale, and the like. "As prices expand," said Dr. Barnea, "the natural resource base expands. As taxes and costs rise, the resource base declines." If we want more oil, we won't get it by taxing domestic oil production.

The Soviet Union's contribution to the UN report was neatly summarized in a *Wall Street Journal* editorial:

> What does the Moscow Academy of Sciences think? At the Austria session, Russian scientists Nesterov and Salmanov reckoned the crude oil resource base at a bit over 12 trillion barrels, or several centuries worth of the stuff. The Russians, by the way, make our 1,001 Years of Natural Gas editorial look puny. By counting hydrosphere gases—natural gas dissolved in oceans, underground water, ice, rivers, lakes and swamps—they figure the planet contains something like 350 billion trillion cubic feet of natural gas. That's 20 million years worth, conservatively, give or take a year.

By 1978, a new humility had quieted all the fashionable predictions of running dry. An Irving Trust study acknowledged that little could be said for sure about 1985. "For 1980–82, however, where supply projections are based on the development of known oil reservoirs, we can make the reasonable judgment that supplies will be abundant and that oil prices (in real terms) will likely fall between 1978 and 1982." While OPEC supplied almost 67 percent of world oil in 1974, Irving Trust estimated that this figure declined to less than 56 percent by 1978 and could fall as low as 42 percent by 1985. A far cry from the CIA fears of soaring prices and slavish dependency. The growing realization that the administration had given up on oil and (especially) natural gas perhaps as much as a few centuries too soon became acutely embarrassing.

Some of the scandalous efforts of the Carter administration to suppress the good news, though generally unsuccessful, are worth describing. The Energy Research and

Development Administration did a study called MOPPS, which estimated that we would be awash with natural gas if the price were allowed to rise to about $2.25 per thousand cubic feet—far less than the going price of an equivalent quantity of heating oil. A price of $2.25 would make economic some 230 trillion cubic feet of inferred reserves, 285 trillion cubic feet from Appalachia, 600 trillion feet from Western "tight sands," and 200 to 300 trillion feet of coal-seam methane (the stuff that often endangers coal miners). At somewhere between $2.50 and $3, which is still competitive with today's heating oil, the MOPPS study figured we could also tap 20 to 50 thousand trillion cubic feet of geopressured methane gas, dissolved in water deep beneath the Gulf region. Altogether, this is enough gas to last between 1000 and 2500 years at current rates of consumption.

The administration wasn't about to have its austerity plans upset by such insubordination, so it borrowed from George Orwell's *1984* and attempted to discard the MOPPS report down the "memory hole." The following notice was sent to libraries by the U.S. Government Printing Office:

ATTENTION
DEPOSITORY LIBRARIANS:

The Department of Energy has advised this office that the publication *Market Oriented Program Planning Study (MOPPS), Integrated Summary Vol. 1, Final Report, December 1977,* should be removed from your shelves and destroyed. The publication was shipped on S/L 10,558 (2nd shipment of February 7, 1978), under Item Number 429-P (El.18:0011/1 (D). We are advised the document contains erroneous information and is being revised. Your assistance is appreciated.

Sent back to the drawing boards, a new batch of ERDA researchers came back with a slightly more pessimistic forecast. Sent back again, they finally managed to get potential gas supplies down to "only" twice as much at $3.25 as at the President's proposed ceiling price of $1.75. And that included only conventional sources, not geopressured methane.

Not content with confiscating books, the administration progressed to purge dissidents. Dr. Vincent McKelvey, director of the U.S. Geological Survey for six years, committed the administration's cardinal sin—candor. Speaking in Boston a couple of months after the President announced his energy taxes, Dr. McKelvey outdid the first MOPPS study by estimating that 60 to 80 thousand trillion cubic feet of gas may be available from the Gulf's geopressured zones. At the low end of the estimate, noted Dr. McKelvey, this "represents about ten times the energy value of all oil, gas, and coal reserves of the United States." Moreover, he added, "a large amount of oil is still to be found in the United States." Dr. McKelvey, needless to say, quickly lost his job as one of the nation's top experts on mineral supply availability.

If hiding domestic energy and inventing phony shortages in Russia wasn't enough, the administration tried to downplay the enormous new oil and gas discoveries in Mexico. Note this early exposé from the *New Republic:*

> The US government has been keeping a secret with enormous implications, but now it's out: Mexico apparently has petroleum reserves of 150 billion to 200 billion barrels, making it an oil power potentially greater than Saudi Arabia. . . . Two Administrations have concealed this information from the American people and from Congress, ap-

parently to avoid undermining energy policies premised on scarcity.

To put it bluntly, there is no energy crisis, no imminent exhaustion of oil and gas even within this country, much less throughout the entire world. The whole notion is a grand deception, a massive fraud. What we have is not a sudden disappearance of natural resources, but a monumental calamity of government regulation.

Had we not hamstrung our domestic oil producers—the overwhelming majority of whom are small venturers, not giants—the energy problem would not exist. Our regulation of our own oil producers and their subsequent inability to pump oil and gas is what transformed the OPEC nations into classic marginal suppliers able to dictate their price. The American people's reluctance to accept this fact is a misfortune of potentially tragic consequences, and the reluctance of so many in public life to refrain from demagoguery and admit the truth is a scandal.

As is true of so many of our present difficulties, our energy problem is exacerbated by our own forgetfulness of essential facts: *Energy is a renewable resource as long as the sun shines. Any motion, anything able to be burned, is a potential source of energy. The earth is not stingy, but bountiful. Resources become scarce only when human ingenuity falters, as it is faltering now because of discouragement by government.*

Actually, we don't even know what the next generation will regard as a natural resource, any more than our ancestors knew what we would do with petroleun, uranium, and bauxite. Substances become resources only when the human mind figures out ways to use them to make something that consumers value.

To be sure, other policies also contribute to our energy troubles. Our confused environmental regulations consistently promote wasteful demand while discouraging supply. Industrial pollution laws pushed industries and utilities out of coal and into artificially scarce natural gas and imported fuel oil. The Federal Coal Mine Health and Safety Act of 1969 shut down 272 mines in ten days and eliminated 25 percent of deep-mine production. Yet, the accident rate went up. The absence of clear environmental standards encouraged seemingly endless legal challenges which delayed construction of the Alaskan pipeline and nuclear plants by several years, and virtually halted offshore oil drilling and the construction of refineries.

Ironically, these actions in the name of "environmental concern" pose a greater potential threat to safety and the environment than would orderly development of domestic energy. For example, by being forced into importing more crude oil and natural gas, we have increased the risk of tanker oil spills and liquid natural gas explosions. By prohibiting surface mining of low-sulphur Western coal (despite provisions to repair any damage to the land), we have forced more men down into dangerous mines to bring up air-polluting high-sulphur coal. And price controls on natural gas have discouraged production of that uniquely clean fuel, and virtually forced its replacement with more nuclear power—a result that disturbs some of the strongest apologists for continued controls on gas.

None of these things, however, caused a "shortage" of oil and natural gas. A shortage always means that consumers want to buy more at some specific price than producers want to sell at that price. If the price were higher initially, consumers would want to buy less and producers would want to sell more, and the shortage would disappear. Without the interference of price controls, the myriad rules and regulations that normally increase demand and restrict supply would simply have increased oil and gas prices, but the prices would have come back down as new supplies came on stream.

But the Federal Power Commission has controlled the wellhead price of natural gas sold to interstate pipelines since 1954, and domestic crude oil has been under some sort of price control since the Economic Stabilization Act of 1970. *The inevitable result was that demand outran supply at the controlled prices, leaving a gap that could only be filled by larger and larger imports.* That put foreign oil producers in an enviable bargaining position. Professor Paul MacAvoy of Yale has estimated that controls on natural gas prices alone had already created a natural gas shortfall by 1972 which was the equivalent of 1.8 million barrels of oil a day. Most of that gap was filled with Arab oil. And the consequences of this government-created gap were at least as large as the peak impact of the Arab embargo.

Decontrolling the price system would provide the incentive to properly conserve energy resources and to develop both energy-saving technology and increased supplies from familiar and exotic sources. It would also provide the incentive and funds for private stockpiling of oil against a possible embargo, and for private research and development. But the government's response to the nation's increased dependence on an unreliable foreign cartel has instead been to extend price controls to new oil and to roll back the total price; to extend price controls to intrastate sales of natural gas; to seriously consider breaking the energy industry into ineffectual fragments; and to compel taxpayers to pick up the pieces (with subsidies and stockpiles) left by this systematic demolition of our energy industries.

It is a tribute to the boldness of thousands of independent oil producers, who drill four out of five wells, that they have not yet been totally paralyzed by the uncertainties of price controls. Like Lucy holding the football for Charlie Brown, the government keeps offering price incentives then yanking them away (after the drilling starts). The price of newly discovered oil was controlled during most of 1972–74, decontrolled in late 1974, rolled back in 1976, and so on. In April 1979, the administration again invited Charlie Brown to drill, this time on the promise of phased price decontrol beginning in 1980, *after* Congress passed the President's proposed "windfall" profits tax. Either way, the President offers producers no added incentive to risk time, money, and expertise on domestic exploration. The upshot is that we will continue to become more dependent on imported energy into 1980.

In the same way, the government has been reneging on its promises to natural-gas producers. Natural gas has heretofore been subject to controls only when piped across state lines, so that prices within producing states have been uncontrolled. The uncontrolled intrastate market had boomed; the controlled interstate market has already given us life-endangering shortages in the winters of 1976 and 1977.

On October 19, 1976, candidate Jimmy Carter wrote this message to the governors of Texas, Louisiana, and Oklahoma: "The decontrol of producers' prices for new natural gas would provide an incentive for new exploration and would help our nation's oil and gas operators attract needed capital." However, in the plan he pushed through Congress in 1978, President Carter did the opposite, extending natural gas price controls to the intrastate market—thus spreading the misery—and continuing controls indefinitely. His reasoning at the time, contrary to the MOPPS study, was that higher prices on new gas would *not* yield more gas, *and* that they would create huge "windfall profits" for gas producers. How gas producers could make huge profits on new gas they supposedly wouldn't find was never explained. In 1979, the President finally accepted the idea that the incentive of higher profits would bring forth greater energy supplies. But on the grounds that those profits would probably be spent by oilmen on buying hotels or real estate, he demanded such "windfalls" be taxed away!

Actually, decontrolled gas would lower energy prices to the consumer for several reasons. First, gas prices in the previously uncontrolled U.S. markets have been well below the cost of Mexican or Canadian gas, or liquefied natural gas from Algeria. Substituting U.S. gas for costly imports would be a bargain. Second, about 80 percent of the consumer's gas bill is actually the cost of operating the pipelines; when price controls create a shortage the pipeline cost per unit of delivered gas goes up. Third, with more gas there would be less necessity for more and more households and businesses to be forced into substituting more costly electricity or imported heating oil.

In the case of oil, there are likewise strong reasons to doubt that holding down domestic crude oil prices has lowered the price of products made from crude, such as gasoline. A Rand Corporation study provides evidence that since prices are set on the margin (by the last unit bought), holding down the *average* cost of crude oil just redistributes income from crude producers to refiners and distributors. Even if that study is wrong, which I doubt, decontrol would boost gasoline prices by no more than six cents a gallon—a good deal less than President Carter's proposed standby added gasoline tax of up to fifty cents.

Oil and natural gas provide over three-fourths of this nation's energy. While other sources can supplement oil and gas, there is nothing on the horizon that can replace them in the next decade or two, even if the economy could bear the huge cost of converting to different fuels.

The General Accounting Office, the Congressional Budget Office, and the Office of Technology Assessment all doubted the feasibility of the administration's proposed massive conversion to coal, given the severe restrictions on mining or using the stuff. Most of our low-sulphur Western coal is on federal land, and there has been a moratorium on new coal leases since 1971. The Clean Air Act amendments of 1977 also require the use of coal scrubbers—a kind of filtering system for smokestacks—that will cost the economy as much as $8 billion a year by 1985. Scrubbers corrode quickly, produce gobs of sludge that is difficult to dispose of, are of dubious effectiveness, and eliminate the incentive to use low-sulphur coal that doesn't need scrubbing in the first place.

Solar power has understandably captured the imagination of many, but there is little hope of its supplying more than a tiny fraction of our energy needs by 1990. (Besides, covering the deserts with acres of solar mirrors is not environmentally more attractive than strip-mining.) Exhaustive studies of the feasibility of providing large-scale solar energy, by California physicist Jerome Weingart, come up with a cost that is equivalent to paying fifty dollars a barrel for oil. Other exotic energy sources likewise face the same problem—they cost too much. Coal-based synthetic oil and gas, for example, can't be produced for less than twenty to thirty dollars a barrel.

Let me offer two axioms by which to judge our energy policy: Since the price of OPEC oil is the "marginal price," that is, what we will have to pay for energy we can't get elsewhere,

1. We should produce all the energy we can up to the OPEC price;

2. We should not produce energy at prices higher than the OPEC price.

The principle here is crystal clear. Let's say you were going to the opera or to a ball game. You get to the concert hall or the stadium, reach in your pocket for your tickets, and discover to your chagrin that you have lost them. Just then two ticket scalpers approach. One offers you a ticket for double the box-office price, the other offers a ticket of the same quality for five times the box-office price. Forced to the choice, which would you buy? Citizens have the same choice to make when government offers to replace thirteen-dollar-per-barrel OPEC oil with exotic processes that produce energy at prices equivalent to twenty, thirty, or fifty dollars per barrel.

Yet when it comes to following our two axioms, the Carter administration's proposals, like all post-embargo energy legislation, fail both tests. We keep domestic oil and gas prices below the OPEC price, while we lavish subsidies and tax breaks on non-competitive forms of energy or conservation. In effect, we tax the cheapest and cleanest forms of energy and subsidize the most costly.

The administration's April 1979 proposals for decontrolling oil prices were a marginal improvement at best. Decontrol remained too gradual, too complex, and therefore too uncertain to form the basis for needed investments in exploration. Federal and state taxes and royalties already claim one-half to two-thirds of any resulting increase in producer profits. The Carter administration would impose an additional tax of 50 percent on whatever is left, again using the proceeds to subsidize high-cost energy sources.

It is not hard to find the source of pressure for more and more taxpayer-financed energy investments that no sensible private investor would dream of touching. "The big attraction of government funding," as *Business Week* explains, "is that it offers recipients the chance to build a major new business at taxpayer expense." Half of the money for Exxon's latest coal-gasification plant, for example, came from the government. And Gulf Oil has graciously proposed to spend $50 million for a plant that would turn coal into oil, if taxpayers will simply venture $450 million on the deal.

Once in operation, however, these white elephants are seriously threatened by decontrol of the prices of conventional oil and gas. The proposed pipeline to bring in Alaskan gas would be impossible unless that Alaskan gas is permitted a price of $3.50 per thousand cubic feet. With decontrol, Texas and Oklahoma could easily provide gas at a much lower price. And much the same applies to a proliferation of uneconomic projects that have a vested interest in continuing the regulatory ban on giving OPEC any competition.

Representative David Stockman has neatly exposed the threat in *The Public Interest:*

> In the name of oil-import reduction, an energy "pork barrel" is now emerging that will make the traditional public works and farm commodity programs look· trivial in comparison. The Department of Energy was recently cajoled into financing a $500 million commercial-scale coal-liquification plant in the Congressional district of the Chairman of the House Commerce Committee. This plant will indeed increase the use of West Virginia coal. But the fuel oil produced will cost East Coast consumers (or the taxpayers) at least $20 per barrel—50 percent more than the alleged monopoly OPEC price. Moreover, this is only the proverbial camel's nose under the tent. The northern Great Plains delegations will push for subsidized coal-gasification plants, the Rocky Mountain delegation for shale plants, the New England delegation for bio-mass-conversion facilities, the Corn Belt for gasohol plants, the Sunbelt for solar credits and subsidies, the fiberglass industry for insulation subsidies, the oil and gas states for restoration of petroleum tax subsidies, the nuclear lobby for expanding subsidized development of uneconomic breeder reactors, and the "soft" technology people will lobby for "appropriate-scale" windmills. The effect of all this "pork trading" will be to burden the Congress with decisions it has neither the competence nor need to make, and to burden the economy with multibillion-dollar excess costs and resource misallocations which will only further stifle our seriously declining prospects for economic growth.

Press reports describe the next phase of President Carter's war on energy as an open invitation to raid the energy pork barrel. "The new phase," says *Business Week,* "stresses increased production from other fossil fuel sources, especially those of unconventional or synthetic origin." The government would, according to *Business Week,* guarantee high prices for some unconventional energy sources, possibly force consumers to use costly synthetics, and "offer loan guarantees, tax credits, accelerated write-offs, or direct federal subsidies." This candy store is being built by an administration that freely describes its critics as "special interests."

Let us ignore for a moment, as the government has for years, our ability to increase American energy independence through decontrol of the domestic energy industry. It is far better to import more oil and gas from non-OPEC countries, if necessary, than to force firms and households in the U.S. to pay more than the world price for energy, either directly or through taxpayer-financed subsidies. A policy of self-reliance at any cost, autarky, is a sure recipe for stagnation. Our industries will not be able to compete effectively in world markets if forced to use costly exotic energy sources, to pay taxes to subsidize such projects, or to adopt costly gadgets to limit the environmental damage from switching from gas to coal. The administration's argument—that such a policy of putting U.S. industry at a disadvantage would strengthen exports and the dollar—was obviously the exact opposite of the truth.

The 1978 energy legislation, although it did away with most of the administration's onerous energy taxes, was profoundly disappointing. Natural gas, which was a minor side issue in the original Carter proposals of April 1977, became the centerpiece of the new law. The fading promise of decontrol was pushed out to 1985, while the immediate prospect was for far more control.

As many of us argued on the floor of Congress, the only result of the natural gas "compromise" of 1978 has been to compromise the future of America's energy supplies. The so-called deregulation actually extended regulation for the first time to the intrastate market. Twenty-five percent more gas will be regulated with the bill in 1985 than without it. *It has been estimated that as many as half the 10,000 independent explorer-producers—who find nearly two-thirds of the natural gas reserves in the United States and drill over 85 percent of the producing gas wells —could be forced out of business by the costs of keeping up with the paperwork and lawyers' fees required by the law.* This is hardly the way to assure additional supply or greater competition in the industry.

The law established *twenty-three different price categories* for newly discovered natural gas, based on proximity to other wells, well depth, commencement date of drilling, underground reservoir date, arbitrary selling prices, costs, and contract provisions. The law imposes on the Federal Energy Regulatory Commission (FERC) the responsibility of determining the gas price for each well— all 165,000 of them, and the 11,000 added each year. Provisions of the bill are purposefully vague or contradictory from one section to another—the intent was to appeal to all groups—and left to the bureaucrats and the courts to sort out. FERC, with a 20,000-case backlog already, realizes how bad the compromise will be in practice. Sheila Hollis, director of the Office of Enforcement, said in a memo, "The office has concluded that the proposal is so complex, ambiguous, and contradictory that it would be virtually impossible for this commission to enforce it in a conscientious and equitable manner."

The administration argued that more energy regulations would improve our balance of payments and strengthen the dollar. But energy costs did not cause the balance-of-payments problem. That problem and the decline of the dollar did not begin with the quadrupling of OPEC oil prices in 1973. Our trade surplus rose from $1.7 billion in 1974 to $18.4 billion in 1975, and did not go into the red until late 1976. Even then, increased oil imports contributed to only 17 percent of the increase in imports. All other industrialized countries have the same increased oil import cost, if not more. Japan imports four-fifths of her energy, but her currency is in much better shape. Why? Japan controls inflation and so the yen rises while the dollar falls.

The only remaining rationale for continued controls was to lower the price of gas for those lucky enough to evade the resulting shortage. Even this promise was wiped out by a provision that was intended to shift the cost of higher priced gas to industry—perhaps so that workers could stay home in comfort after their factories were forced to shut down. This was the so-called "incremental pricing" scheme. Instead of spreading the cost of higher-priced gas among all consumers of gas, the compromise would make the industrial-commercial users pay the increment, or price above the basic price. You would expect residential users to pay less, right? Wrong. The higher price has encouraged the industrial-commercial users to convert from natural gas to imported oil, the next cheapest fuel. This will have three adverse effects. First, the smaller number of industrial-commercial users will mean that the remaining gas-using firms have to pay even higher prices and pass them along to consumers in higher prices for their goods and services. Second, with fewer commercial users, residential users pay a higher transmission cost per unit for the pipeline, which is about four-fifths of their gas bill. Third, the shift to oil from natural gas only increases the foreign energy dependence the compromise was supposed to cure.

Ironically, the Carter administration did a complete flip-flop in late 1978—switching from the idea that the nation could not extract more natural gas at any price to the opposite notion that the destructive 1978 natural gas bill would somehow generate so much production that we could afford to renege on a promise to buy gas from Mexico. On April 29, 1977, the administration's energy plan had told us that, "It is doubtful that even substantial price increases could do much more than arrest the decline in gas production." By January 24, 1979, Energy secretary James Schlesinger was urging state commissioners to hook up more new homes to gas, and urging industry to again switch back to gas. But the unexpected surplus of natural gas had already begun to be undone by the so-called gas compromise of 1978. The number of U.S. drilling rigs in operation dropped from 2,385 to 2,088 in a few months, and a *New York Times* report (March 26, 1979) attributed an 8 percent decline in drilling activity to "confusion over Government pricing policy on natural gas."

The energy strategy of the Carter administration has been cloaked in grand phrases about "conservation" and "fairness." In reality, all the taxes, subsidies, prohibitions, and regulations are clearly designed to benefit some firms and individuals at the expense of others. What passes for "conservation" is often just cutting back on one use of energy so that somebody else can get more, or get it cheaper.

Professor Henry Rowen of Stanford saw clearly through the Carter energy plan:

> The Plan can reasonably be viewed as a massive income-redistribution scheme: away from oil refiners, against those who favor large cars; in favor of residential users of oil and gas and opposed to industrial use; in favor of the northeast versus the southwest; in favor of coal miners and owners in the east (which has high-sulfur coal) and opposed to those in the (low-sulfur) west; in favor of those who have delayed insulating their homes (who can now receive money for what it pays them to do anyway) and away from people who live far from the job and drive to work. All in the name of fairness.

When something is desirable and limited in supply, there are only two practical alternatives to the price system as a rationing device—letting government officials decide who gets what, or lining up to receive things on a "first come, first served" basis. Neither alternative distributes good efficiently—that is, toward uses that consumers themselves value most highly. Rationing by either political preference or the queue is also an invitation to waste and bribery. First place in line naturally tends to go to those with the most political clout. Talk about "fairness" of such systems is either naïve or intentionally deceptive.

What about "conservation"? Here too we are victimized by our national forgetfulness about matters we once understood. It is no favor to our descendants to hoard something that could otherwise be turned into something of greater value. Suppose that back in 1900 our great-grandparents had stockpiled oil instead of selling the oil then and investing the proceeds in manufacturing. This would have been a preferable alternative, estimates a study for the International Institute for Economic Research, *only if by 1975 the price of oil had exceeded $12,- 900 a barrel!* The same study concludes that enforced long-term conservation of a variety of minerals would have impoverished both past and future generations throughout this century. If we leave the future a legacy of oil instead of more and better factories, the oil may well be of as much use to our successors as whale oil to us.

Yet this is precisely the intention of the Carter administration, on a grand scale. To be sure, the process did not begin with the present administration. Between 1968 and 1974, the amount of public land closed to exploration and development of mineral wealth was increased from 17 percent to 67 percent for hard-rock minerals and 73 percent for leasable minerals like coal, oil, and gas—that's the size of all the land east of the Mississippi River, and 400 times the land area ever used for mineral mining in the United States! President Carter has outdone even that. After the Senate would not lock up public lands in Alaska from exploration and possible development, President Carter and the Secretary of the Interior invoked "emergency" conditions and closed off development of 121 million acres—56 million acres permanently, and the rest for at least three years.

"To put this in perspective," editorialized the *Wall Street Journal,* "prior to his action, about 9.5 million acres had been set aside [permanently] under the act since it passed in 1906." The 56 million acres are "roughly New York state plus most of New England," the *Journal* noted. "The 121 million acres equal the land area of the eastern seaboard states from Maine down to North Carolina."

Professor William H. Dresher testified recently on what can be lost by setting aside public lands (and private lands, through regulation) after a cursory examination of their potential based on currently available technology:

> Let me give you an example of this. In 1920, the U.S. Geological Survey reported upon an area south of Tucson regarding its mineral potential. Following this report, the Commissioner of the General Land Office, in 1922, instructed the Registrar and Receiver in Phoenix that the land ". . . is hereby classified as non-mineral in character." A close examination of an aerial photograph made in 1937, 15 years later, shows no evidence of mining activity in the area covered—an area of some 525 square miles of land— 15 miles across by 35 miles long. Yet, today that very area of the photograph hosts five major copper mines which, in 1976, produced some $456 million in copper—over 327,- 000 tons, or 12 percent of the copper consumed by the entire country in that year. If a withdrawal action had taken place based on the Commissioner's 1922 instructions, think of the copper, jobs and tax dollars which would have been lost to our society by now.

"It is hard to think of any mineral deposit whether it be metal or fuel which doesn't contain mineral worth of at least $200,000 per acre!" Professor Dresher said. "What other usage, be it timber, agricultural crops or recreation can possibly match this value to society?" In many cases, the mineral product is recyclable forever, and the land is reclaimable for other uses.

President Carter's inability to resolve the energy issue is also linked to his obsessive worry that some American energy producer might profit from producing more energy. Oil company profits average only around 5 percent of sales. To make that nickel margin look like "war profiteering," President Carter felt compelled to give a figure for total oil company sales and pretend that it was after-tax profits. Then, in a televised address, the President said, "The question is who should benefit from those rising prices for oil already discovered." That was misleading, since even new oil and gas would be held below the world price under the Carter plan, and the definition of "new" was quite restrictive. Still, a choice between windfall profits and windfall taxes is not so clear as it seems. The administration's original proposal for taxing away the difference between the controlled price and the world price amounted to a 100 percent tax on alleged excess profits—something unprecedented even in times of war. While a quota or tariff on oil imports is like imposing an embargo on ourselves, the President's proposed tariff (wellhead tax) on domestic production was even less defensible.

When the price of a house or farm soars, nobody suggests that the tax collector should get the whole gain. When the salaries of Congressmen go up, nobody suggests paying the higher salary only to attract new Congressmen, not to retain old incumbents. Why should the ownership of oil be so much less secure than ownership of land or human skills?

Any spurt in profitability from decontrol would only partly compensate for the government's previous expropriation. Ending an official ripoff is not the start of a private ripoff, but the beginning of fair and sensible response to artificial scarcity.

James Schlesinger, head of the bloated Energy Department, knows perfectly well that decontrolled oil and gas prices would vastly increase supplies, eliminate wasteful demands, and give OPEC some healthy competition. He said as much to the Atlanta *Journal* on May 21, 1977: "True, Adam Smith's 'invisible hand' would probably accomplish these economic goals rather efficiently. However, this classical economic process, ideal though it may be for allocating resources, is not the most effective arbiter of social and political interests."

What exactly did Dr. Schlesinger mean by "political interests"? That was stated clearly in an article he wrote way back in 1968 in the *Journal of Law and Economics:* "The tool of politics (which frequently becomes its objective) is to extract resources from the general taxpayer with minimum offense and to distribute the proceeds among innumerable claimants in such a way as to maximize support at the polls."

Our energy and conservation policies should give all Americans a voice and a share. Our public and private lands should be open to many uses, so that the greatest number of people benefit—not just hunters from back East who can afford to charter airplanes to reach the roadless Alaskan wilderness. Our government should not decide that giving subsidies to the buyers (and, indirectly, the manufacturers) of fiberglass insulation is all right, but dismiss natural market incentives for producing more domestic energy as "war profiteering." An undistorted price system permits both producer and consumer to express their values freely and efficiently. It benefits everyone by providing the right amount and types of conservation. There is no escaping the fact that physical energy is a substitute for human energy—which increases our productivity and living standard. It cannot be official policy to reduce energy use regardless of consequences or costs, when freeing the price system can and will increase the value produced with each unit of energy. The government always has a role in safeguarding the future—but that means everyone's future. Once our government realizes that we are all in this *together,* it will find that its most pressing task is to remove many of its own obstacles to the common goods of quality and growth.

While we're concerning ourselves with energy, there is a related matter that merits our attention. Of all the sins committed in the name of conserving energy, none is quite so annoying and counterproductive as the government's heavy-handed plans to cram the American people into tiny cars. Our cars are being designed in Washington to accomplish a variety of inconsistent objectives at the highest possible cost and inconvenience to the American consumer.

The war against the American automobile must be motivated by more than saving fuel. After all, passenger cars only account for about an eighth of all U.S. energy consumption, and new cars are only about a tenth of that eighth (or less than 2 percent). So nothing dramatic can suddenly be accomplished by shrinking new cars. Besides, people are driving fewer miles than before, and increases in motor fuel consumption have slowed from 5 to 6 percent a year before 1973 to about 2 percent since.

No, the battle against autos is more ideological than practical, and more divisive than helpful. It pits communities with taxpayer-subsidized mass transit against cities that are spread out or wide open rural spaces. It pits big families against small, traveling salesmen against those with a short commute.

The inconsistencies are ludicrous. The first pollution-control gadgets increased gasoline consumption by 300,-000 barrels a day. Average gas mileage of new cars dropped from fifteen miles per gallon in the 1950s, when tiny cars were rare, to 12.9 miles per gallon in 1974. We needed better air pollution standards. But the government didn't stop with standards; it required specific devices to meet the standards. The newer catalytic converters spray foul-smelling and possibly dangerous sulphuric acid in the air, and get hot enough to start forest fires. It requires about 8 percent more crude oil to refine a gallon of unleaded gas for the new cars, and they often ping badly even on that costly fuel.

The push for safer cars has also had to face difficult trade-offs. Larger cars are still unquestionably safer for occupants, but it has become unfashionable to say so. Mandated oversized bumpers and structural beefing-up add significantly to auto weight and fuel consumption, and any savings of repair costs in low-speed accidents may be offset by the fact that the new bumpers are more costly to replace in high-speed accidents. A seat belt and shoulder harness are apparently safer than air bags for those who buckle up, but the greater risk and cost of air bags may nonetheless be imposed on everyone because some don't fasten their safety belts. The dangerously troublesome seat-belt interlock system added $107 to the cost of 1974 cars before the public outrage allowed them to be disconnected at additional expense.

The constant buffeting of changing laws and regulations has had a devastating effect on U.S. automakers, particularly Chrysler and American Motors. On August 8, 1977, *Newsweek* reported that it still wasn't clear whether or not Detroit would be allowed to sell its new cars: "If the 1977 exhaust-emission standards are not extended through 1978, Detroit would simply have to quit making automobiles—or pay a fine of up to $10,000 a car for violating the law."

"The cost of these federal edicts," noted *Business Week,* "hits Chrysler harder than its wealthier competitors. . . . Yet even as Chrysler shows some signs of catching up to its competitors in the first round of federally mandated vehicle redesign, it must gird for the second one. And it is largely the cost of that overhaul that lies behind Chrysler's burdensome $7.5 billion financing campaign." General Motors figures that it takes a $1 billion investment to save a half-mile per gallon; smaller rivals can't handle that sort of expense.

Congress can force the automakers to make tiny cars, but it can't force the people to buy them. Last December, Ford was right on the verge of violating mandated average mileage standards because the company's Continentals were selling beautifully while smaller models were not. If Ford's fleet dropped from an average of 19 miles per gallon to 18.9, the company could be fined about $12.5 million. The message? Don't build what consumers want, build what Washington wants them to have.

President Carter railed against the "gas guzzler." Our laws will soon fine firms for making big cars and tax consumers for buying them. But a large family of large people really does need space. Many have responded to the demise of large sedans and station wagons by buying vans that use far more fuel per mile. The EPA rates a full-sized Buick 6 with automatic transmission at eighteen miles per gallon; a stick-shift Volkswagen bus gets only seventeen. We can scarcely ban or even shrink the vans and small trucks, since they have essential commercial uses.

One way of keeping a little elbow room while improving gas mileage is to switch to diesel engines, although they are balky, underpowered, and cost $300 to $900 more. If you travel 15,000 miles a year (10,000 is average), the EPA figures your fuel bill would be $428 in a big Olds 98 diesel with automatic, $438 in a stick-shift Toyota Corolla. (Who's the "gas guzzler" now?) But the diesels emit tiny carbon particles which may (or may not) aggravate respiratory disorders, so diesels may not survive the EPA's latest edicts. Perhaps adding turbochargers to the diesels would meet the air standards, but it would also add another $285 to the price.

One cynical motive for buying a diesel is to protect yourself against political rationing. During the oil embargo, the Federal Energy Administration pushed refineries to produce more diesel fuel and less gasoline. President Carter's proposed gasoline tax likewise excluded diesel fuel. It can be comforting to have the Teamsters on your side.

By 1978, the cumulative cost of Washington's auto engineering had added $666 to the average price of a car, according to Professor Murray Weidenbaum. Those who can afford it are thus blessed with assorted buzzers, plumbing, and gadgets. The rest must drive their old clunkers until the tiny new models become so unappealing that an old big car may command a higher price.

By 1982 or 1983, if current legislation stands, the largest car a U.S. citizen will be allowed to buy will be the size of today's compacts. By 1985, cars are supposed to average 27.5 miles per gallon, which suggests that a Honda Civic will be the norm. Because of switches to costly aluminum and plastic (which require considerable energy to manufacture) plus diesel engines and/or turbochargers, the consumer will pay much more for less. If inflation increases about 6 percent a year, the price of an average car could easily jump from $5,750 to $8,000 by 1983.

Government has no right to dictate in infinite detail how the American people spend their hard-earned incomes. By doing so, we weaken one of the crucial rewards for productive effort—buying a car that meets one's special needs. If energy prices are free to reflect replacement cost, people will have every incentive to conserve scarce resources, including energy. *And each family and firm will adapt according to its own circumstances.* Some may prefer to drive a larger car less often, some may drive a smaller car at a higher speed, some may instead economize on heating or air conditioning. Since politicians cannot know what each person prefers, it is arrogant to decide that one use of energy is "wasteful" while another is "essential"—that motorists must cut back to leave more oil for making plastic bags or polyester skirts. This whole costly experiment in central planning must not be part of our agenda for the future.

8   *Exporting the American Idea*

The United States emerged from World War II as undisputedly the strongest, richest, most influential nation on earth. There was in 1945, by all accounts, a worldwide period of expectation and hope that the United States would use its dominance as the unscarred democratic power to lead the way to a postwar era of peaceful communion. For the fascist Axis had been defeated not just by America the nation, but by the American idea, an idea of democracy, individualism, and freedom that was not only "worth fighting for," but powerful enough to win.

By its very nature, this American idea was inclusive, not exclusive; it was there to be shared. There was in that moment a shining vision of a world of nations united to preserve the peace, with the United States—possessing the atomic bomb—able to guarantee it. There would be the United Nations, the name itself suggesting the hope of inclusiveness, rather than the "League of Nations," which suggested a coalition of elite nations. Most importantly, the United States seemed enthusiastic, even eager, to take on this responsibility—as it had not been prepared to do after the First World War. We even had a clear idea, expressed through President Roosevelt, that our obligation was not to reinstitute the prewar status quo. We would not abide the continued humiliation of the vanquished nations, nor the preservation of our allies' colonial regimes.

Tragically, however, American foreign policy was forced, from almost the beginning, into a framework of defensiveness. To understand this, one must grasp the dichotomy in the American people's postwar desires. More than the people of most nations, Americans understood and cherished political liberty. Yet like the people of all nations, at least most of the time, they sincerely desired peace. But here the people's desire for peace, unlike the case under too many other political systems, gets turned into policy.

Cherishing liberty, and facing reality, we would combat aggression in Greece, Berlin, and most conspicuously, Korea. We would buttress our allies with foreign aid, the Marshall Plan for Europe, military and economic assistance. We shielded our allies by staying ahead in the arms race, and pacified our underdeveloped nations by transferring resources to them—to keep them from "going communist," in the phrase of the time. Because we cared so much for peace, however, we settled into a three-decade-long habit of reaction.

Militarily, there was no alternative: *Democratic nations are not warrior nations.* Pre-emption, "first-strike" wars of tactical advantage are repellent to them. *But this is all the more cause to strike with the greatest weapon in our arsenal—the prospect of general well-being that results from the embrace of American ideas about opportunity, initiative and enterprise.* There has hardly been, in all the years since World War II, an ideological offensive by the United States as a strategy of foreign policy, yet I believe that is exactly what the world was looking for from America after the war, and what it has hoped for from us on more than a few occasions since. It was the responsibility of the United States to share the recipe for prosperity, assisting and guiding those who expressed a desire to experiment with democratic capitalism. That is what other nations—and especially the newly liberated nations of Asia and Africa, and the underdeveloped nations of Latin America—wanted from us.

That isn't what they got. The most likely explanation for the bizarre economic advice they did get is that in 1945 and the years after, though we were confident of our economic and military power, we had quite forgotten their source. *Because of the Great Depression, we lacked confidence in the economic essence of the American idea, though our belief in its political essence remained strong.*

There was then, as in many circles there remains today, acceptance of the illusion that the stock market crash of 1929 and the Depression that followed demonstrated the failure of the private sector. Free enterprise was flawed, ran the argument, because the speculative greed of the capitalist class led to overproduction of goods by this class, and the workers were left without the purchasing power to buy the excess goods. Thus the collapse. The solution, as argued by the Keynesian economists of the 1930s, was for the government to take a direct hand in the process by redistributing surplus production through the government's power of taxation and expenditure.

Roosevelt's New Deal tinkered with this mechanism during the 1930s, but never to the satisfaction of the Keynesians. The financing of World War II, however, seemed to confirm the arguments of the Keynesians. Through the intervention of government to direct and control the war effort, production leaped severalfold, and the mass unemployment of the 1930s ended almost overnight. At war's end, the Keynesians were so vocal in their insistence that government direction of the economy was necessary in peacetime that this idea became embedded in the psyche of America's postwar policymakers.

The starting assumption in this whole scenario was wrong. The stock market crash of 1929 did not result from the overproduction of greedy capitalists and dizzy speculators, and the Depression was not caused by the breakdown of capitalism and free enterprise. In his book *The Way the World Works,* Jude Wanniski has demonstrated beyond any reasonable doubt that it was a political blunder—of the Congress acting in concert with President Hoover—which ended the prosperity of the 1920s by enacting the Hawley-Smoot Tariff Act.

In other words, the level of production was not in "surplus" until the United States raised its tariff wall so high against the rest of the world that they could not afford to buy from us, because they could not sell to us. In this light, the American idea was not flawed in its economic ingredient, but in its political mechanism. President Hoover and the Republican Congress responded to narrow political interests in the United States and inserted an enormous impediment to commerce into the global economy. President Roosevelt chipped away at the tariff wall during the 1930s, but it was the advent of war and the war itself that generated a whole new set of incentives to commerce and production, incentives to save Western civilization from fascism.

The mistaken view of the Depression precluded an "ideological offensive" in the postwar years. Our confidence in our *political* system led us to impose representative democracy on Germany and Japan, to the point of writing constitutions for them. This was fortunate, as it gave these two nations the political strength and ingenuity to *resist our economic advice.* And it even took several years for that to happen—until 1948 in Germany, and until 1950 in Japan. This is because the economic advisory teams we sent to those countries after the war were already infected with the Keynesian idea and counseled state capitalism, with vigorous taxing and spending policies.

Ironically, in 1948 West German Finance Minister Ludwig Erhard imported the essence of the American idea against the advice of American economists, thereby ending the economic crisis that postwar American advice had brought on. In 1965, John Chamberlain could write in his book *The Roots of Capitalism* (a book I gave to my son Jeffrey on his high school graduation):

> Germany has recovered faster than post-1945 Britain simply by *abolishing* controls, rationing, state-directed investment, sharply progressive taxation, and the "fair shares" mentality which insists that all people must be equal in their misery. In West Germany the top progressive rate is around 50 percent; in "rich" America the top rate stood for a long time at 91 percent, and still remains confiscatory in the higher brackets. Yet in Germany, with a relatively low rate of tax progression, the government

has still been able to restore monuments, to take care of its distress cases, and to behave in a generally humane way.

In Japan, which was similarly afflicted by the economic counsel of our advisory teams, dynamic growth did not begin until 1950, when its parliament, the Diet, decided it was time to try the original American idea, the new ideas having brought nothing but stagnation and misery. The great Japanese trading companies we had broken up in 1945 were reconstituted, and the confiscatory tax progressions we had advised were shattered with loopholes to provide economic incentives. As the economy grew and revenues expanded, the government continued to reduce tax rates. Every year between 1950 and 1974 there was reduction in tax rates. The Japanese economic "miracle," like the German "miracle," was nothing more than the non-miraculous result of an American idea American economists had forgotten about.

The rest of the world was not so fortunate. They too looked to the United States for leadership, and they came, innocent as lambs, to Washington, D.C., and the United Nations in New York to learn the secret of economic growth. The steadfast advice they got was to tax and spend, control and direct investment, run deficits, devalue their currencies, limit imports, and push exports. And for the most part our advice was followed, and we wondered through the 1950s why, more and more, the people of the less-developed world became more hostile toward our leadership. We wondered why peasant leaders, suddenly in control of millions of dollars, became corrupted. We wondered why young nations, counseled to develop strong central bureaucracies, became fertile soil for dictatorships. We wondered why we were steadily losing support in the United Nations. We wondered why it was that the competing ideology seemed to be gaining influence and prestige at our expense.

And we came to exactly the wrong answer. I remember as a teenager in the early 1950s, and in college during the middle of that decade, hearing the idea expressed again and again that democratic capitalism, perhaps even democracy itself, might not be a practical system for the underdeveloped world. A democracy requires the existence of a strong middle class, was another theme. An uneducated peasantry, given the franchise, would simply vote themselves the resources of the tiny productive class, falling prey to demagogues, and there would be no growth. Maybe all these new little countries required a strong hand, a benign dictator who would make wise decisions on behalf of the rabble. These enticing excuses were mouthed by Democrats and Republicans alike.

At times the doubts about democracy extended to the United States itself. I also remember hearing the idea expressed in the 1950s, especially around the time the Soviet Union orbited Sputnik, that the Soviet leadership enjoyed certain advantages over the U.S. leadership. Soviet planners, after all, did not have to brook dissent, while U.S. officials had to contend with obstinate labor or obstinate business. The suggestion was that in a race against a totalitarian power, democracy was handicapped by having to carry the burden of consensus.

In 1961, President John Kennedy took the United States on its first "ideological offensive" as leader of the free world. We would race the Russians to the moon. We would try to root Fidel Castro out of Cuba and, failing that, ponder his assassination. We would announce an "Alliance for Progress" with Latin America. We would dispatch fresh-faced college kids to help people around the world as part of a "Peace Corps" with a positive mission, though spreading the American idea was seldom a part of it. (Pathetically, some of the youngsters spent their time urging local populations to rebel against social conditions that were the result of policies suggested by American "experts.")

The main event of this ideological offensive occurred in Vietnam, where the Kennedy administration genuinely attempted to export the political half of the American idea, as well as economic prosperity. In this "social laboratory" of South Vietnam, the United States would develop an Asian showcase, a "Third Force"—neither capitalistic nor communistic—that would be so successful it would attract the rest of the underdeveloped world in emulation. But as did most of our efforts to help others, this one neglected the American idea's economic element. Our hapless plan was to funnel military assistance into South Vietnam on the express condition that its political leadership refrain from doing any of the things the United States did in growing from an agrarian nation into an industrial power. We advised "land reform," which meant confiscation of land holdings. We advised steeper taxes on businessmen and the well-to-do in order to finance social programs designed by State Department personnel who knew little about economic growth. We advised currency devaluations and inflation to stimulate commerce, and government controls to regulate it. And when the economy got sicker and sicker, our State Department agreed it was because the political leader of South Vietnam, who had been scrupulously following our blueprint, had not been following our blueprint with sufficient fervor. We withdrew our support from him, he was assassinated, and we spent 50,000 American lives before throwing in the towel on this phase of a hideously inept ideological offensive.

It speaks volumes that by 1975 the nation that had pressed hardest for the postwar emancipation of colonial territories, that had provided billions more in aid to other countries than had any other nation, that had indeed pushed hardest for the international assembly that became the United Nations, had become a butt of ridicule among some of that institution's pettiest tyrants. For the first time, even our *political* system was coming under attack by the UN representatives of fledgling dictatorships and oligarchies. What might have been just another case of static, defensive reaction—or shamefully feigning indifference—was transformed into a successful ideological offensive by the oratorical craftsmanship of our UN Ambassador, Daniel P. Moynihan. After three decades as leader of the free world, American leadership was finally rediscovering the crux of the American idea: human freedom, the most powerful tide in the history of Western civilization—*which by its very nature is concerned fundamentally with individuals, not collectives.*

To his credit, President Carter pursued a global human rights policy for a time, and as best he could. Yet even when he was at his best, his pleas could not help but have a moralizing, busybody tone. Better than nothing, to be sure, but a long way from being convincing to a now too cynical world. What began as a flame in 1975, was barely a spark by late 1978, when President Carter damaged his credibility on the subject by the manner of his renunciation of Taiwan. Long before that Christmas week fiasco, however, it seemed that President Carter had run out of interesting things to say about human rights.

There is an explanation for this. As long as the human rights issue remained one of comparing this nation with others—as in our refusal to be lectured on decency and justice by noisome petty tyrannies—we had a credible and compelling argument, and one that we ourselves understood. We had faith—especially when eloquently reminded—in our democratic institutions, our *political* institutions, at least when placed side by side with those of other nations.

Yet because our formulation of human rights neglected what I will call the "economic dynamic" of human rights, the issue soon degenerated into tallies of what country had how many political prisoners, and how they were treated. For it was not to form a trinity that our American founders included "the pursuit of happiness" as an inalienable human right—a right so fundamental that it was beyond the power of any individual to relinquish it or any government to take it away. They had in mind precisely the economic dynamic and knew that without it all other rights are jeopardized, and even ringing defenses soon turn hollow. Once we recall the mutually dependent relationship of human freedom in political affairs and human freedom in economic affairs, we will be able to make the strongest possible argument for our way of life.

I consider it a given that all people desire peace and prosperity, and that therefore the greatest national service would be to offer ideas, policies, and leadership that bring closer the goals we all proclaim. The ultimate task of American leadership is not and has never been the submission of the Soviet Union, or the People's Republic of China, or Cuba, or anywhere else. The policy of containment, as initiated by President Truman, was not simply a "power politics" solution. As Truman said, as he launched the containment policy in his "Truman Doctrine" speech: "The seeds of totalitarian regimes are nurtured by misery and wont. They spread and grow in the evil and soil of poverty and strife. They reach their full growth when the hope of a people for a better life has died. We must keep that hope alive."

The problems with this containment policy arose when we misunderstood the essence of America's original formula for success. And it remains—no matter how many times we lose sight of it—the advancement of ideas that are by their nature so attractive, magnetic, and inclusive that people of all nations will choose them for themselves.

I am suggesting a frame of mind for American foreign policy, one comparable to a greatness of soul. I do not mean that the United States should disregard military danger or Soviet ambitions any more than a positive approach to crime in the streets would mean retiring the police force. The point is rather that a dynamic frame of mind enables us to think more clearly about policies (foreign or domestic) that reach for consensus and are not content with coalitions and power blocs and those power politics "solutions" that seem quickest and easiest and end up bloodiest.

Consider our reaction to the communist regime in Cuba. The power-play solution was, first, an invasion to get rid of Castro; failing that, his assassination; failing that, a blockade of the island to strangle the economy. None of this worked, because our heart wasn't in it. We are not, at bottom, an invading, assassinating, embargoing kind of people.

What should we have done instead? We should have surrounded Cuba with a dynamic, prosperous Caribbean economy. Decreased Castro's allure by increasing the allure of the private economies in the Caribbean relative to his brand of public economy. *In fact, had we been an active exporter of the American idea to the Caribbean in the 1950s, Castro would have had to rely entirely on naked Soviet military power, without the genuine appeal for change which arose out of Cuba's severe economic hardship.* Cuba today is a shining example of the failure of American leadership in the terms I have described. There was not, as far as I can tell, any attempt at all by the United States in the postwar period to discourage Cuba's political leadership from destructive economic policies.

The pattern was the same for Cuba as it was for the rest of the Free World. The Keynesian economic professors who dominated our best universities uniformly advised state capitalism as the surest prescription for economic growth. The ruling politicians of the client countries, whether left or right, would be advised to borrow heavily from the New York banks or the World Bank or the International Monetary Fund, in order to build economic "infrastructure"—highways, roads, harbors, water systems, industrial plants, schools, hospitals. Once all these good things were in place, economic production and prosperity would follow, they said, and the loans would be paid off by taxing the citizenry, which by then would presumably be in a position to pay taxes.

It was all theoretically idyllic; but as it turned out, the

advice from Uncle Sam was pitiful, literally pitiful. The only parts of the scenario that went according to plan were the parts about borrowing money and raising taxes. The almost universal experience was that some of the money would be spent on the designated work, and the lion's share of it lost to corruption, inefficiency, and waste. In most cases the "foreign aid" had strings attached by the U.S. government, requiring that funds be spent in the United States with American contractors. This provided a built-in constituency in the United States that pushed for more loans. The major American banks became part of this international pork barrel, brokering loans to Latin America, Africa, and Asia—and taking their cut. But the sad truth is that American taxpayers, whose generosity underwrote the grants and subsidized the loans, paid but a small part of the tab. The really big bills were slipped under the doors of the world's poorest people—the Third World peasant and worker—who in the end will have to pay off all this debt.

After a full quarter century of this pitiful process, the Third World debt to American and international banks has run to more than $200 billion. And because the tax rates have been put up so high in the Third World countries in order to make payments on the debt, the local incentives to produce and save and work and invest are crushed to a vanishing point. The tax rates then yield insufficient revenues to meet the debt schedules, and the countries borrow more from the banks to pay on those old low-interest loans with new high-interest money. How can anyone not sympathize with the Third World pleas for debt moratoriums? It is no wonder at all to me that the United States is viewed as an "imperialist" power in so much of the world, no wonder that "Yanquis" are invited to go home. It is a wonder that so few young countries have gone the way of Cuba—at least they could get out from under their debts, as Cuba did, by simply defaulting on loans. It is a tribute to the appeal of democratic institutions (and to these nations' self-respect) that this temptation is resisted. These new nations await political leaders who will be able to find a way out of this dispiriting cycle of debt and taxation while invigorating democratic institutions.

The way out, I believe, is being demonstrated by Carlos Romero Barcelo, the governor of Puerto Rico. The Puerto Rico experiment now under way can be a pattern for the entire developing world. I will let Malcolm Forbes, Jr., tell the story by quoting him at length from his column of October 2, 1978, in *Forbes* magazine, a column entitled "Look What's Happening in Puerto Rico":

> Since taking power 20 months ago, Governor Carlos Romero Barcelo has been vigorously chopping away at the island's taxes. Two weeks ago he announced that a 5% surtax enacted back in 1954 would be abolished, and that next year there would be a 10% cut in all income tax rates. . . .
>
> In the 1950s and 1960s Puerto Rico experienced a German-like economic miracle. But in the early 1970s the economy sputtered and then, with the quadrupling of oil prices, economic growth disappeared.
>
> The initial response of the Commonwealth's government compounded the island's problems. At the behest of a blue-ribbon committee of American economists, bankers and financiers, Puerto Rico raised taxes in 1974. The theory was that the increased exactions would reduce inflation

and dampen consumer spending, which was considered "bad." Business investment was regarded as "good," and there were no new levies there.

The program was a flop. The economy continued to "sit down," as Puerto Ricans put it. In 1976 voters threw out the incumbent governor and his long-dominant party.

Thanks in large part to Romero's tax-cutting moves, Puerto Rico's economy is perking again. After experiencing no growth in 1974–76, it expanded almost 5% last year and should do even better this year.

Romero's plan is to bring Puerto Rico's top marginal tax rate on personal incomes down to 50 percent by 1981 from the 87 percent level (reached at $100,000) when he took office. As his strategy unfolds, I believe we will see such positive results in the Puerto Rican economy—in terms of productivity, employment, growth, and general well-being—that the island will point the way for the rest of the Caribbean and Latin America, then for the developing world of the Eastern Hemisphere as well. For it is a sad fact that with rare exceptions, the Third World is now afflicted with progressive tax rates on personal incomes so high and steep that U.S. rates seem tame by comparison.

In the Asian subcontinent, for example, the rates are murderous in their disincentive effects. In Bangladesh, the 65 percent rate is encountered at a mere $6500 annual income. In India, the 60 percent rate is paid at $9800, and 60 percent is reached in Pakistan at $7000.

In Africa, the rates are almost as bad, and often worse. Tanzania, for example, claims 95 percent of all income in excess of $2386 annually, Kenya 70 percent of income over $1000, Gabon 85 percent of income over $16,700,

Ghana 75 percent of income over $12,522. The one really bright spot in all black Africa is the Ivory Coast, where wise political leadership resisted the advice of American economists and bankers in the 1950s, and rejected the bogus debt-and-inflation path to prosperity. The Ivory Coast thus enjoys the lowest tax rates on the continent—with a top rate of 37.5 percent, encountered at about $20,000. As a result, the Ivory Coast has a vibrant, bustling economy, with more uniformity in its prosperity than any other country of black Africa.

In Latin America as well, personal tax rates are extremely high in most nations, although the top rates are usually encountered at slightly higher income levels than in Asia or Africa. Thus the same opportunity exists throughout the entire Third World to generate a higher level of economic efficiency and personal well-being, simply by slashing away at tax rates now so high they mine little or no government revenue but bury hope.

These incredible barriers to expansion present a moral imperative: The United States has a responsibility to undo the damage of its counsel over the past quarter century. Resistance will come from the usual quarters, the economists and bankers and financiers who arranged the Third World's financial calamity. The International Monetary Fund, the headquarters and club for this group, and the major bulwark of resistance, continues even now to spread the gospel that austerity and currency devaluation are the keys to success. Yet when the bankers and financiers see palpable evidence that the mortgages they hold on the Third World economies stand a far better chance of being paid by bustling economies than by economies in chains, resistance will wither.

A new foreign policy frame of mind would mean

American commitment and assistance to projects such as the longtime dream of Ivory Coast President Felix Houphouet-Boigny for a West African customs union. Such an enterprise, combining the dozen nations of West Africa in a common market, monetary union, and tax union, would loose the incredible intellectual, physical, and natural resources of black Africa, and lift the entire continent out of its present tensions, stagnation, and despair. And a rapidly expanding West Africa would serve as an economic counterpole to the Union of South Africa, a magnet that would draw out of South Africa the most able and enterprising black workers. That sort of economic "sanction" will force an end to racial discrimination a lot quicker than will foreign embargoes and military threats. It is an example of the way exporting the American idea can win victories without risking lives.

I believe we have this opportunity within our grasp, a chance to offer the kind of global leadership the world expected of us in the first place.

And offer it we must. As much as we might be tempted to focus all our attentions on our own country and our own economy, we can't escape the fact that there really are no purely domestic solutions. We can take all those actions, repeal those unnecessary regulations, cut all those tax rates necessary to get the United States back on the track of the American dream, but unless we see to the buoyancy of the rest of the world, our troubles will be frequent.

There is a higher reason as well: that history not say that in the American epoch the world was a seething, despairing place. We have an idea that fathers prosperity and hope. It is time to offer it, not selectively, not grudgingly, but with confidence to a world that needs the human dream that grew up in America.

9 *Strategy for Defense*

There is really only one significant direct threat to America's national security, and it comes from the Soviet Union. The threat is primarily a military one, for the Soviets have built up an arsenal that some consider to be the most powerful in history. What makes this arsenal so dangerous is not merely its vast amount of firepower but the nature of the governing elite that has its fingers on the trigger.

Communist rule has always been established by means of force or revolutionary takeover involving the threat of force, and never in history has a major communist government been overthrown, deposed, or, needless to say, voted out of office. From this historical pattern we see why the Soviets place such a high premium on the use of military force and other means of police coercion. Force or the threat of force is the primary way they succeed in attaining their goals.

Today we see them directing a military buildup unprecedented in modern peacetime history. This buildup has covered every conceivable aspect of military preparations: equipment, manpower, and money for every military department, for civil defense, and for the scientific, technical, and industrial infrastructure. As former U.S. Arms Control and Disarmament Agency director Fred Charles Iklé has noted, this effort could not be the result merely of bureaucratic inertia or of policies lacking clear intent. Since the mid-1960s, the Soviet military buildup has included:

- four new land-based strategic missiles with four or five new systems to be tested over the next few years while the United States has added none, and will not deploy a new land-based missile until 1987 at the earliest
- an operational anti-satellite system for which the United States has no counterpart
- the production of an average of more than 3,000 tanks per year, or more than five times the number of tanks the U.S. has produced in the same decade
- new mobile long-range ballistic missile systems for which the U.S. has no counterpart
- 800,000 troops added to its armed forces—this addition to the Soviet Army alone is larger than the entire U.S. Army
- the production of 1800–2000 military aircraft annually or about three times the U.S. production rate
- more than a dozen types of tactical aircraft with range and payload characteristics not significantly inferior to the far less numerous inventory of U.S. tactical aircraft.

The evidence of the Soviet's single-minded obsession with military power could easily fill this volume. What one can conclude is that the scope of Soviet investment in

land, sea, and air forces for waging regional or interconti-
nental warfare has been increased drastically by every
measure in the past decade, and we have not met the
Soviet threat with a determined effort of our own.

To make matters worse, the Soviets also possess a military doctrine (i.e., the body of thought that directs the
operation and employment of military forces) that is fundamentally different from ours. We in the United States
believe in deterrence and thus have adopted what is
called a second-strike doctrine: American strategic forces
are designed to withstand a Soviet first strike in numbers
sufficient to perform a retaliatory strike that would guarantee destruction of enough Soviet civilian targets to
deter the Soviet strike in the first place.

Since the mid-1960s, our second-strike nuclear posture
has relied on a doctrine of deterrence known as much for
its acronym as for the doctrine itself, Mutual Assured Destruction (MAD). If nuclear war were to erupt, we hold
that both sides would be destroyed. But for well over a
decade, there has been no incontrovertible evidence that
the Soviets share this policy. The Soviets simply do not
accept our idea that mutual destruction would be the only
outcome of nuclear war. They believe that victory is possible in such a war. They reject MAD because, according to
one prominent Soviet analyst of American military affairs,
it implies an "a priori rejection of the possibility of victory," which leads to "moral disarmament, to disbelief in
victory, to fatalism and passivity." The recent patterns of
Soviet strategic deployments indicate their actions corre-
spond to their words. The tremendous explosive power
and the large numbers of Soviet nuclear warheads indicate that the Soviets are interested in acquiring a capabil-

ity to attack and destroy a major fraction of American strategic forces as opposed to urban/industrial targets. By the early 1980s, the Soviets will be able to destroy 90 percent of the U.S. land-based Minuteman force (1000 are currently deployed) with fewer than 300 of their own ICBMs, leaving more than 1000 ICBMs in reserve to deter a U.S. retaliatory attack.

In the past decade, the Soviet conventional (non-nuclear) forces, particularly those in Europe, have become a formidable force that threatens Western Europe and ultimately the U.S., both politically and militarily. Soviet armed forces, unlike their NATO counterparts, are organized along unapologetically offensive lines. The essence of Soviet military training and organization is preparation for offensive operations. In this the Soviets are utterly explicit. The directives contained in Soviet training manuals, many of which have been translated and published in the U.S., are fully confirmed by evidence from Soviet military maneuvers.

The Soviet Union has developed its own variant of World War II blitzkrieg tactics for its conventional forces. The Soviets have eliminated traditional infantry divisions from their armed forces, replacing them with either tank or mechanized divisions suited to high-speed offensive warfare. This change has required a massive building program in armored vehicles; there are now more than 45,-000 tanks assigned to 170 Soviet Army divisions, with additional thousands in reserve. More than 5000 tanks and armored personnel carriers are being produced each year, about four to five times the number being produced in the United States. Soviet tanks deployed with their divisions (i.e., not counting those held in reserve) now number more than four times the total number available to the United States Army.

Similarly, the notion of a swift and massive conventional strike has required a vast increase in the procurement of tactical aircraft to permit Soviet forces to strike at the rear area air bases and supply depots that are an essential component of American military power, particularly in Western Europe. The Soviet Union produces 1800 to 2000 military aircraft per year, one-fourth of them tactical bombers, or about four times the U.S. production of military aircraft. Although the image of Soviet aircraft being crude and technologically unsophisticated was apt until the early 1970s, we may no longer take much comfort from such an assumption. New Soviet aircraft such as the Foxbat (MiG-25) and the Flogger (MiG-23/27) series of fighter-bombers are very much up to date in terms their ability to perform in modern combat. The comforting palliative about the Soviet Union emphasizing "quantity over quality" is no longer true—they have dramatically upgraded the quality of their armed forces while maintaining the ancient Russian practice of piling weapon upon weapon in seemingly endless quantities.

The massive accumulation of weaponry in Eastern Europe is aimed at the center of the diplomatic interest of the Soviet leadership—Europe. Their forces deployed in the nations of Eastern Europe are far larger than would be required as an occupation force (if that were sufficient justification). Indeed, more than 100,000 troops have been added to the Soviet deployment in Eastern Europe in this decade; tactical nuclear delivery systems have been drastically increased (while the U.S. was withdrawing its delivery systems); tank and artillery holdings by each of the thirty-one Soviet divisions there have been increased by 40 percent; and three new tactical missiles will soon be deployed. These massive forces are organized, trained, and equipped to initiate a conflict with little warning; surprise and concealment are crucial elements of Soviet military preparations, as their military maneuvers so clearly demonstrate. The Soviets have the ability to carry out an unreinforced attack in Europe with what is now a high prospect of success.

The delicate public consensus in most of the nations of Western Europe makes it unlikely that they would invest more resources in defense than they now do as a proportion of their gross national product. Hence, as Soviet military power grows, there is a grave risk that some of the NATO nations may seek a form of political accommodation with the Soviets on unfavorable terms, thus exposing other nations of the NATO alliance to greater military risk. Another no less dangerous prospect is a shaking of the political resolve of our allies induced by the diplomatic "weight" of Soviet arms, sometimes referred to as "Finlandization." We have already experienced the impact of the threatening of Europe's oil supply by the OPEC nations that caused most of the NATO nations to prohibit our use of bases on their territory for the resupply of Israel in 1973. The subtle effects of looming Soviet military superiority in Europe may take years to accumulate sufficiently to cause our allies to seek to "adjust" to the change, but we should not delude ourselves into thinking that such an adjustment cannot happen.

Perhaps most telling is the way the United States has acted with respect to the Soviet threat at sea: We have abandoned even the pretense of meeting the Soviet naval threat that will loom in the next decade. The naval shipbuilding program proposed by the outgoing Ford Administration in 1977 was cut in half. Despite the advice of every senior naval officer, the modernization of the only area of naval warfare where we hold a decisive advantage, large aircraft carriers, has been terminated. Instead, only a single new carrier will be built before the end of this century, and that will be one with half the capability of the carriers we have most recently produced. Indeed, production of naval carrier-based aircraft has been slashed to the point where soon only nine of our twelve aircraft carriers can be equipped with aircraft! The decisions on naval shipbuilding are of momentous importance because they force the United States into a situation where it must operate *as if* it were a land power, and so we are deprived of one of our most powerful assets, the ability to project American military power abroad by sea. It is that ability the United States has had through naval forces to project its power abroad that the Soviets have sought most diligently to prevent.

For most of its history the United States has relied on its naval forces as the principal instrument for the protection of its interests abroad. In the modern era, this has meant, in effect, the ability to operate tactical aircraft in support of ground (Marine) forces ashore. This has made the role of the aircraft carrier (and the ships associated with it in a carrier task force) the central element of an American military presence beyond the reach of our land bases. It is this ability that has been the focus of the Soviet countereffort.

Until the mid-1960s, the Soviet Navy was primarily designed for coastal defense to prevent attacks on the coastline or shipping from hostile naval forces. As the Soviets expanded their investment in naval forces, their effort was directed toward types of ships that could best be used in the anti-carrier role. The type of navy they have today, and will have in substantially greater numbers in the next decade, reflects this choice. Soviet naval forces can be most simply described as a "first-strike" navy, for their ships are designed to carry almost twice as many weapons as their American counterparts, but without a significant capability to reload their weapons for extended conflict. Soviet ships lack magazine capacity to carry many reloads and, in general, cannot be reprovisioned at sea because of the great weight and bulk of their weapons. Thus, the Soviets have deployed a force that can launch a massive salvo of cruise missiles against a carrier task force in hopes of inflicting knockout damage. If the Soviet Navy is able to do this, it will have succeeded in its mission. Those who are complacent about the growth of the Soviet Navy suggest that its failure to build large aircraft carriers similar to ours illustrates how far behind our own the Soviet Navy is. But, in fact, the Soviet Union has energetically built a Navy which meets *its* foreign policy objective—to prevent the U.S. Navy from projecting American power abroad—but we have not maintained a Navy which meets *our* objectives.

The Soviet military threat's effect on U.S. security is compounded by the increasing accumulation of Soviet diplomatic influence around the world as a consequence of the growth of Soviet power. This extension of Soviet influence has been accomplished in a variety of ways including:

- the organization of communist coups or insurgencies in a number of nations in the developing world
- the covert or overt support of Communist elements of "national liberation movements," particularly in the developing world
- the support of terrorist movements, either directly, as in the case of such terrorist organizations as the Palestine Liberation Organization, or indirectly, through third nations such as Libya
- seeking to deny Western access to raw materials in developing nations as in the case of the Soviet encouragement of the Cuban/-Katangese invasion of Shaba Province in Zaire which disrupted the West's primary source of cobalt. Only a few months before, the Soviets had engaged in massive purchases of cobalt on the international market.

The United States announced its policy of détente with the Soviet Union at a time which coincided with the largest buildup of Soviet military power since World War II. Détente could have made a contribution to encouraging less belligerent behavior on the part of the Soviet Union if it had been carried out under circumstances where the United States would have built up her own military forces to offset the Soviet effort. Lamentably, détente has become an instrument for the encouragement of the most dangerous and threatening Soviet international behavior much to our disadvantage.

American policy in the détente environment has given the Soviets a perception of weakness. Our failure to take decisive steps to improve our strategic nuclear arsenal in the face of a fourfold increase in Soviet nuclear strength in a decade suggests weakening American resolve. Similarly, the Soviets see the divisive debate over the division of government expenditure between defense and domestic welfare needs as a symptom of the "crisis of capitalism" that ultimately threatens both domestic social cohesion and the ability to finance an adequate defense establishment. Yuri Davydov, a Soviet commentator on the United States, has argued that the manifest collapse in American resolve is a "recognition" by our political leadership "of the failure of the American path of development."

As a result of international developments, we are perceived by the Soviets as having lost the will to employ military power in defense of our interests in recognition of the shift in the balance of power to the Soviet Union. It is the American recognition of growing Soviet military power that has compelled the United States to seek a relaxation of tensions ("détente") with the Soviet Union.

By embracing the policy of détente we have taken the risk out of Soviet international adventurism. In the latter half of the 1970s, the Soviets have sponsored successful revolts in Angola, Mozambique, Ethiopia, Afghanistan, and South Yemen. This has been accomplished by the Soviet airlifting of Cuban troops, military advisors from Soviet bloc nations, particularly East Germany, and the extensive use of Soviet intelligence personnel. The successful revolts have been rapidly exploited by the ruthless suppression of potential sources of opposition. In the past, such behavior by the Soviets was deterred by the certainty that the United States would act to prevent it as we did in the 1950s and early 1960s. American unwillingness to jeopardize the continuation of Soviet-American détente has allowed the Soviets to accelerate their efforts to penetrate the developing world.

The forlorn hope that a "code of détente" (ground rules governing Soviet-American behavior) could be established that would dissuade the Soviets from their adventurism in the developing world has contributed to our reluctance to respond to the Soviet threat. Most fundamentally, détente has obscured the genuine and profound differences between our free and democratic society and the Soviet's odious totalitarianism. By obscuring the profound differences in values between our two societies, the significance of the incipient preponderance of Soviet military power is withdrawn from view, only to emerge with unanticipated ferocity in some unavoidable future crisis when we are so militarily weak that we are unable to defend our own interests.

In describing the size and scope of the Soviet threat, one begins to appreciate the cumulative effects of more than a decade of disinvestment in defense in the United States. Little by little, the enormous advantage that the United States had throughout the postwar decades—our ultimate "insurance policy" against the uncertainties of international affairs—has vanished to the point where there are few decisive areas of military potential in which our lead is sustainable under current or planned programs. The situation is by no means beyond recovery, but the risk of further delay in finding a remedy for the inexorable decline of our military potential is perilous.

I believe there are nine steps our defense policy must take to ease the short-term threat the Soviets will present in the decade ahead:

1. *Resources.* There is no escape from the necessity to devote more resources to our national defense. Defense expenditure has declined from over 8 percent of our GNP in 1968 to about 4 percent today. Although we spend

more on defense today than we did a decade ago, when the effect of inflation is considered, we are actually spending less. This would not be such a serious situation were it not for the fact that the Soviet threat in almost every category amenable to measurement has increased severalfold in the past decade. Our strategic forces are living off the legacy of a massive investment in the late 1950s and early 1960s, while our conventional readiness has not yet recovered from the damaging failure to modernize U.S. forces during the Vietnam conflict. We cannot expect to counter Soviet strength by increasing our investment by 3 percent per year when the Soviets increase their expenditure by 4 to 5 percent per year. Such a disparity is a formula for a dangerously weak U.S. defense posture for many years.

An increase in resources devoted to defense must be done for several reasons in addition to that of simply acquiring greater military strength. Such an increase would constitute an important demonstration of resolve, reversing the impression the Soviets have acquired over a decade or more of neglect of our defense posture. Moreover, such a demonstration of resolve will provide an incentive to the Soviet leadership to moderate their behavior in the international arena, and will encourage them to be more amenable to reasonable arms control arrangements. Inadequate investment in defense deprives the President of the policy alternatives he needs to meet the wide variety of foreign policy contingencies which may emerge over the next decade.

2. *Change our arms control posture.* Perhaps the most damaging aspect of our entire national security apparatus is the manner in which arms control policy has become a

substitute for defense policy. I strongly believe that arms control can contribute to national security, but it can never do so if our policy perceives arms control to be an alternative to investment in defense. Today, needed investment in our strategic nuclear forces is being blocked in the hopes that the Soviet Union will voluntarily abandon the advantage our failure to modernize provides them in the Strategic Arms Limitation Talks. As a result, we are now suffering the worst of both alternatives. We neither improve the capability (and hence the deterrence value) of our own strategic forces, nor are we in a diplomatic position to provide the Soviets with an incentive to agree to strategic arms limitation. In a similar fashion, we have allowed our friends and allies to suffer grave risks by restraining the sale of arms abroad, while the Soviets are engaged in building up the military power of most of our adversaries around the world.

3. *Strengthen U.S. alliances.* The United States is allied with the most technically advanced industrial nations of the world today. As a result, joint action with our allies can make a great contribution to our mutual security interests. Our foreign policy in recent years has, however, acted to weaken the bonds of our alliances severely. We have unilaterally abrogated a solemn alliance with the Republic of China, and are withdrawing our military forces from the Republic of Korea despite advice to the contrary from every allied nation in the region. In the Strategic Arms Limitation negotiations, we have agreed to terms which will exclude from the agreement several strategic systems which threaten NATO (SS–20).

The error has been compounded by the acceptance by American negotiators of "non-circumvention" language in the strategic arms agreements which will make it difficult to sustain unfettered military cooperation with our allies. The agreements will prevent us from transferring military technology to our allies that is denied to the United States (especially ground- and sea-launched cruise missiles). This tragic error will weaken the structure of U.S. alliances severely in the next decade if policy changes are not made before then.

4. *Support pro-Western forces under Soviet-sponsored attack.* Throughout the postwar period, the U.S. came to the aid of many nations whose independence and territorial integrity came under attack from Soviet-sponsored assault. This policy helped preserve the peace in Europe, the Middle East, and Northeastern Asia in the 1940s and 1950s and deterred subsequent adventures by the Soviets in areas where the West stood firm. Our record has been far less impressive in recent years as the victories of communist-supported armies in Angola, Mozambique, Ethiopia, and Southeast Asia attest. Only with a resolute and determined effort to support Western allies can we expect to deter ever bolder assaults on the nations of Africa, Asia, and South America by Soviet-sponsored insurgents.

5. *Enhance the U.S. industrial mobilization base.* The latent power of the United States is not our armed forces, but rather in our scientific-industrial infrastructure with its potential to meet our military needs in a crisis. But fundamental changes in the American industrial structure have served to weaken our industrial base as we move from a manufacturing to a service economy. Basic industries central to military production, such as steel, chemicals, petroleum, and aluminum, have been run down as the perverse effects of U.S. tax and environmental policy have made it uneconomic to maintain large basic industrial plants in the U.S. Our industrial base has

been even further eroded by governmental action to the point where mundane military equipment cannot be produced in quantity under current government programs, much less those required in time of crisis. A 1978 Department of Defense exercise known as "Nifty Nugget" revealed serious weaknesses in our ability to exploit our potential scientific-industrial base in a time of crisis. There has also been a considerable slowdown in scientific and technical innovation in the United States due to the declining investment in research and development. This observation applies not only to military research and development (which has declined steadily in non-inflationary terms since the mid-1960s), but in the private sector as well, where the rewards for the economic risks of investment in advanced technology are diminishing under tax policies that penalize savings and investment. Serious planning and investment in our industrial mobilization base will be necessary if the United States is to have a credible disincentive to further Soviet arms buildup.

6. *Recognize American security interests in the developing world.* The nations of the developing world, with their rapidly growing economies, are frequently at crucial geographic points in the world, or possess great mineral or agricultural potential that the Soviets would find advantageous to deny to the U.S. and the industrial nations of the Western alliance. The tendency after Vietnam has been to ignore the nations of Asia, Africa, and Latin America, in effect leaving a vacuum which the Soviets have swiftly sought to fill. To recognize American interests in the fate of the developing world means that attention must be paid to improving our naval forces, encouraging commerce with developing nations,

and "living with" a higher level of involvement in world affairs.

This involvement should include a role in the defense of the seaborne lifelines of the West, namely those nations whose geographical position places them athwart the crucial passages and straits through which most seaborne commerce passes. The risks of failing to recognize our interests in the developing world are, however, far greater than proceeding down the path of "benign neglect" we have chosen to date. A developing world that is composed of nations predominantly hostile to the interests of the United States is a prescription for the isolation of the United States from the rest of the world in both an economic and national security sense.

6. *Strengthen U.S. intelligence services.* The diminishing margin of safety we now enjoy with respect to Soviet military power makes our intelligence apparatus far more important to our security than it ever has been in the past. Yet, our intelligence capability has never been weaker since the Korean war. Not only is there excessive compromise of intelligence information through "leaks," but our ability to collect information needed for our security has been inhibited as well. The ability of the U.S. to collect "human intelligence" through covert action has been so severely circumscribed by legislative action and executive decision that this low-cost but crucial means of intelligence collection has, in effect, been abandoned. The loss of access to foreign bases has made collection of certain types of intelligence virtually impossible, forcing ever greater reliance on photographic satellites and electronic intelligence collection. Without the energetic pursuit of a covert capability to verify such exotic forms of collection,

policymakers may be reluctant to act in the face of intelligence in which they can only place modest confidence.

We should also understand that our intelligence services have the potential to contribute to the support of U.S. foreign policy objectives through the taking of secret initiatives on behalf of the United States. This capability that produced far more beneficial results in the past than many of its critics suggest has been all but eliminated along with other forms of covert action. We can no longer afford the luxury of gratuitous attacks on our intelligence services and their means of supporting our foreign policy objectives.

8. *Refrain from strengthening totalitarian nations.* The totalitarian nations of the world, with but a handful of exceptions, are those nations in the Communist orbit which seek to acquire Western technology. By the sale of such commodities, we assist in strengthening their military power either directly, when the technology has military applications, or indirectly, when we make it possible for the Soviets, for example, to avoid shifting their military manpower to production by selling them our goods. During the decade of major agricultural sales to the Soviet Union (since the late 1960s), the Soviets increased the size of their armed forces—in spite of a severe domestic labor shortage.

9. *Assume the burden of international leadership.* The United States has not welcomed the role that it found itself in following World War II. Yet this role is not one that can be accepted or dropped depending upon current fashion. Failure to perform well as the free world's leading nation does not mean that the burden will fall elsewhere—it simply means that those who would wrest

power from the non-communist world will have an easier time of it, and those outside communist orbits will be compelled to pay the price.

The American people by and large have been spared the consequences of our foreign policy failures in the past three decades. It is mainly the unfortunate people of Eastern Europe, Africa, Asia, and Latin America who had allied themselves with us who have suffered. Unless the international performance of the United States improves very substantially over what has become the norm in recent years, we shall all bear the burden of failure directly. Since the end of the Vietnam conflict, the U.S. has acted as if it could shed the burden of international leadership without any consequences. In fact, since Vietnam we have witnessed the fall of Angola, Mozambique, Afghanistan, South Yemen, and Ethiopia to communist rule; Iran has moved from an allied nation to one that is no better than neutral and in many ways may be hostile. How many more reverses will emerge in the next few years no one can forecast, but I do know that the United States must become an active leader in international affairs, promoting an international environment conducive to our security, our strength—and ultimately our ideals.

The idea that weakness can be provocative was expressed by Donald Rumsfeld during his tenure as Secretary of Defense in 1976. The notion that "weakness can be provocative" is a property of our failure to invest adequately in defense that too often escapes the notice of those who so vigorously press for reductions in defense expenditure. The logic of Soviet ideology is such that, in the words of Charles Bohlen, a former American ambassador to the Soviet Union, the Soviets will continue to extend their sword until it strikes steel.

The Soviets have not yet struck American steel as they seek to extend their power to remote corners of the world. Reconstruction of the American capability to effectively deter Soviet expansionism rests upon our ability to develop a truly effective military establishment. I have no doubt that the potential vitality of our economy is adequate to meet all of our military requirements. Only unwise economic policy can prevent our economic system from producing resources adequate for what Adam Smith described as the prerequisite for economic prosperity—security.

10   *An American Renaissance*

In 1976, America's Bicentennial Year, like many Americans I found myself absorbed in a fresh discovery and appreciation of our nation's roots and history. I'd always been a history buff, but in 1976, spurred on by a special pride in being a member of Congress, I spent more evenings than usual reading history books and, especially, rereading the early architects of our American experiment. As I reflected on my own experiences in government, my appreciation of the wisdom of the Founding Fathers redoubled. In the Federalist Papers, or in Madison's account of the Constitutional Convention, I'd find political or economic insights that seemed fresher and clearer, more appropriate to my experience in the present, than many of the modern books I had put aside in order to visit the past. Economic strength had to be built on individual freedoms, they knew, and defense was not a fortified line, so much as internal unity and faith in the ideas and institutions of representative government.

More than a century after the Founders, an American

statesman would explain the importance of the principles proclaimed in Philadelphia in 1776 in this way:

> The Declaration of Independence derived its peculiar importance, not on account of what America was, but because of what she was to become. She shared with other nations the present, and she yielded to them the past, but it was felt in return that to her, and to her especially, belonged the future.

Yet on the threshold of the 1980s, that quotation, from Theodore Roosevelt, would seem to many antiquated and chauvinistic. Young people especially have little feeling these days, as they did when I was young, of an American obligation, growing out of an appreciation of our nation's special history, to advance the future of the world. It isn't that any other nation or even group of nations has displaced America in this sense, staking a claim on the future, but rather that the job is vacant.

The world, though, needs leadership—some one nation, big enough, strong enough, and confident enough to accept the responsibilities of greatness. And by "leadership" I do not mean power or wealth necessarily, and I certainly don't mean mere strength to dictate a course of action. I mean the ability to rally others to a goal, a cause, or an idea. If there isn't such a genuine leader, history demonstrates that some pretender will try to fill the vacuum.

Needless to say, I am not simply or even primarily speaking about regaining a sense of confidence lost in Southeast Asia. The erosion of America's confidence is more fundamental than that, which is why so much of this book has been devoted to economic policy. For in the last dozen years, concurrent with our blunders and setbacks abroad, we have felt our economic strength draining away, and more importantly we have had imprinted on the national consciousness a sense of futility about our ability to regain economic vitality. We not only doubt our ability to conquer the inflation that saps this vitality, but our leaders accept it as a way of life and project "acceptable" rates of inflation into the next century. We are asked to accept the idea that America's dynamism has run into the resource limitations of the earth, and the kind of growth that once was a way of life for Americans is no longer possible. This is obviously not a vision conducive to renaissance and renewal. It leads rather to abdication of a primary leadership role for the United States, as in our willingness, even eagerness, to see the U.S. dollar decline as a world currency.

If all we had learned in the last dozen years had to do with economic policy, though, we wouldn't have learned very much. In fact, most of what we learned through trial and error about economic policy was simply a relearning process. Viewed in this light, there is nothing startlingly new about economics that any of us has learned, nor are there any new ideas in this book. When you tax something, you get less of that thing. When you create too much money, each unit of that currency loses its value. Again and again, for thousands of years, the sages repeat these messages, but we only seem to learn how eternal these truths are after periods of experimentation trying to improve upon them. It is important, crucially important, that we as a nation went through this exercise, as in the same way we had lessons to learn in our dealings with other nations. The 1960s and 70s have been decades of learning we won't soon forget. Now, and in the 1980s, if we seriously want to build an American renaissance, to reclaim a future that ought to belong to us, we can do so with this rediscovered wisdom.

I think, though, that our greatest rediscovery has to do with politics. In the process of finding out that you can't impose solutions, you not only learn the limitations of power. You also learn an appreciation of democracy. I remember discovering, after I had changed professions, one of the most important differences between quarterbacking and politics. When you're a quarterback, you are trying to impose a solution. When you go into the huddle to call a play, you don't ask for opinions. You don't listen to the crowd. You make up your own mind and expect execution. As a politician, that doesn't work. You have to listen to people, because it is their interests you are attempting to represent. And if you want to call a play, it's not enough for you to expect mechanical execution. You have to explain what it is you're trying to do, and in the course of doing so, you find yourself getting new questions, new information that may cause you to alter direction. You might call this learning process on my part the "democratization" of Jack Kemp.

In this same way, I think, we went through this kind of passage as a nation in these last dozen years, insofar as the rest of the world is concerned. We learned that the world expected leadership from the United States. It did not want us to just impose solutions, but to use our dynamism, our wisdom, our vantage point to listen for information from all sources, and at least make an effort at reaching a consensus.

Instead of calculating our interests almost solely on the basis of whether a government is nominally for us or against us in international forums, which was the litmus test of foreign policy for a quarter century, there is now a heightened awareness that our interests are also bound up with the people behind these governments. I remember Irving Kristol recollecting a conference he attended in the mid-1950s, about the future of the emerging nations of Africa. All the participants but one, he said, argued that the people of these countries were not prepared for representative government, that they were too vulnerable to demagoguery. The recommendations were uniform in advocating strong, educated leaders to keep these impulses in check. But one speaker, whose voice was drowned out at the meeting, argued that the only common sense in the new countries was at the grass roots, and there would be trouble if the anointed elites would import ideas and attempt to impose them without consulting this common wisdom.

It seems to me that describes nicely the American situation today. There are stronger democratic processes in the United States than almost anywhere else in the world, but I think we have learned in this last decade that we could have used more. The Proposition 13 movement in California was a perfect example of what I mean. The political leaders of California could not solve the structural conflicts between state and local tax policies, and the people were needlessly suffering as a result. Because California has an initiative system, the people themselves could and did break through this political inertia, with the "Prop 13" voter initiative. In advance of the vote on June 6, 1978, Los Angeles mayor Tom Bradley predicted "a destruction of local government as I know it" if Proposition 13 passed. Economists like Walter Heller forecast "chaos." But the people of California knew what they were doing in their direct appeal for a solution to that structural conflict. There was no destruction, no chaos after the initiative was approved. The politicians were forced to adjust the tax structure. They did so. And the economy and revenues improved.

One country of the world that has more democracy than the United States is also, I believe not coincidentally, more peaceful and prosperous than the United States. In Switzerland, the citizens can initiate legislation at the national level and also nullify legislation through the referendum. In the December 18, 1978, issue of *Fortune,* there was this account:

> Says Willy Linder, economic editor of the *Neue Züricher Zeitung:* "The Swiss remains unselfish and sensible enough to vote at times in favor of issues that seem to be against his or her self-interest. Yet, in the long run, these attitudes have contributed to Switzerland's economic and political stability."
>
> During the past three years, for example, the Swiss, by margins generally exceeding 3 to 1, have decided in referendums *not* to cut the work week from forty-four to forty hours, *not* to levy special taxes on the rich and high-salary earners, *not* to grant Swiss workers a say in the management of Swiss industries, *not* to reduce the qualifying age for admission to Switzerland's generous old-age pensions, *not* to allow the central government to raise funds to counter domestic economic downtrends, and finally *not* to allow the central government to run deficits.

This is an impressive statement about the common sense of the Swiss, but I think people around the world are basically no less sensible. If avenues to express that sense do not exist, though, policies of government cannot really reflect the common sense of the people. The time is right, I think, for the United States to take the lead in a fresh global wave of democratization that demonstrates the efficiency of government forms that rest on the wisdom of ordinary citizens. The most fundamental change we could make, I think, is to provide for a national initiative, through an amendment to the Constitution patterned after the successful example set by Switzerland. A bill that begins the process of constitutional change was introduced in the 95th Congress by Senators Hatfield of Oregon and Abourezk of South Dakota. Hearings are promised in the present 96th Congress, and I would hope the issue would receive enough attention and support as a result of the 1980 elections to make the "Voter Initiative Amendment" a reality in the early part of the new decade.

The amendment, which really extends our First Amendment right to petition the government for redress of grievances, would enable citizens to place a proposed law on the ballot once they successfully collected sufficient numbers of signatures. As presently introduced, signatures equal to 3 percent of those last voting for President (about 2½ million) would be required to protect against frivolous use of this mechanism. Votes would be taken on initiative questions only in off-year elections, and a majority would enact the proposed law. Changes in the law could be made by a two-thirds vote of each house of Congress in the first two years after enactment, and by a majority thereafter. Neither constitutional amendments nor calling up the militia nor declarations of war would be subject to the initiative.

The initiative has been used successfully at the state level since the turn of the century, when South Dakota became the first state to authorize it in 1898. The District of Columbia and twenty-three states presently authorize the initiatives, and in eighty years have used it to decide about 1100 issues. There are movements in other states to enact it. At the federal level, though, is where government urgently needs to tap the wisdom of the electorate. "One thing is certain," Senator Hatfield said last year. "The American people are searching for some means of expression at the national level." I agree.

There is and will be powerful resistance to the idea from Washington and the "establishment," from those who have power and do not wish to relinquish it. Their argument, like all arguments against expanding democracy, is that the people are incapable of deciding issues of great moment. Syndicated columnist Pat Buchanan, a supporter of the initiative amendment, put it well when he wrote: "Unlike 1789, 1977 is a year of mass education and mass communication. While the people are still unequipped to make day-to-day decisions of government, they are as qualified to pass upon individual laws as upon the individual men who make them."

I feel as strongly as I do about this reform because I believe it goes to the heart of our national malaise. Somewhere along the line we lost the focus on the individual, the family, and the neighborhood that was once the heart of the American Dream. Political leadership turned away from confidence in the citizen as an individual, in the family as the bedrock of a free society, and the neighborhood as a basic unit in the democratic framework. Attention instead turned toward Washington, and to an infinite

variety of grandiose programs and plans that were supposed to lead or command us to a better life.

Among politicians and their academic advisers, the pre-
vailing attitude toward the American people became paternalistic, even condescending. The people were supposedly as uncharitable as they were gullible, and were
not to be trusted with even the simplest decisions about
how to earn, spend, or give away their money. It was
preferred that most earnings should be taken from them,
and spent on their behalf. We simple folk have to be
strapped into automobiles designed in Washington, and
surrounded by buzzers and air bags; we should be offered
fewer varieties of breakfast cereal, and need to be warned
that mouthwash will not cure the common cold. In one of
our federal agencies, the wise men even proposed that
vitamins should be made prescription drugs, because people were buying too many of them.

Local governments and voluntary organizations were
likewise quickly dismissed as stupid or incompetent by
those awed by the federal government's seemingly unlim-
ited power to tax and command. "For years," wrote Richard Cornuelle in *De-Managing America*, "we have encouraged the federal government to tax away money that
would otherwise have nourished nonfederal institutions
and then smugly pointed out that nonfederal institutions
obviously had a waning capacity for social responsibility
because they were taking less and less of it." Revenues
and responsibilities thus became increasingly politicized
and centralized, with the result that people feel they have
lost control of their government, and even of their own
destinies. True democracy rests on a respect for individuals that has been whittled away by having so many

decisions made by our new clerisy in Washington.

This increasingly heavy-handed intrusion into every detail of American life is based on the notion of social engineering—that people can be systematically arranged and manipulated, like so many pieces on a chess board. Our schools teach that economic progress can be managed from above, rather than that it is created by individual action, by ordinary people who live and love and work, and who alone constitute the essence and purpose of any society and economy. Our news is the news of Washington officials pretending to control the activities of millions of people, activities that they cannot possibly comprehend, much less manage.

"You can command a man to turn a nut on an assembly line," writes Richard Cornuelle, "but you cannot command him to be creative or concerned or resourceful." The ballpoint pen was conceived by a sculptor, two musicians discovered the Kodachrome process, and the safety razor was designed by a traveling salesman. An insurance salesman became one of America's most illustrious classical composers, an insurance executive among its greatest poets. Government cannot command the changes that add vitality to a society and economy; government can only provide a tax and regulatory environment conducive to individual initiative.

The question is thrown back at us: Doesn't the growing complexity of our economy require more intervention, more direction from the center, less democracy? On the contrary, centralized bureaucracy can't cope with complexity, diversity, and change. In "Prometheus Bound," an article in the September 1978 *Harper's,* George Gilder wrote:

The most dire and fatal hubris for any leader is to cut his people off from providence, from the miraculous prodigality of chance, by substituting a closed system of human planning. Innovation is always unpredictable, and thus an effect of faith and freedom.

In the United States today we are facing the usual calculus of impossibility, recited by the familiar aspirants to a master plan. It is said we must abandon economic freedom because our frontier is closed: because our biosphere is strained, because our resources are running out, because our technology is perverse, because our population is dense, because our horizons are closing in. We walk, it is said, in a shadow of death, depleted air, poisoned earth and water, a fallout of explosive growth showering from the clouds of our future in a quiet carcinogenic rain. In this extremity, we cannot afford the luxuries of competition and waste and freedom. We have reached the end of the open road; we are beating against the gates of an occluded frontier. We must tax and regulate and plan, redistribute our wealth and ration our consumption, because we have reached the end of openness.

But quite to the contrary, these problems and crises are in themselves the new frontier, are themselves the mandate for individual and corporate competition and creativity, are themselves the reason why we cannot afford the consolations of planning and stasis.

If it is the fate of the United States to be bound like Prometheus, which I absolutely do not believe, then we should at least permit the *people* of the United States to make that judgment, not the master planners. A new wave of democratization, which would be resisted by officialdom, would break the bonds that are choking off our vitality as a people. Even if the voter-initiative avenue were rarely used at the national level, its presence and its potential would be an added reminder to the planners that power in the United States properly resides with the people of the United States. And our commitment as a nation to extending the frontiers of democracy, I will bet, will do more than all our global lecturing to aid the spread of democracy.

An American renaissance need not await constitutional change, however. While we are working on democratic reforms that will revive the primacy of the individual, we can deal simultaneously with the other crucial issues on our American agenda.

We must have economic growth, at home and abroad, which means we must press ahead to gain the necessary tax and monetary reforms that will permit growth. Government can and must lower marginal tax rates to leave people with a larger share of any added income they earn by contributing to the nation's output. Government can and must maintain the domestic monetary standard—the dollar—by ending inflation, and in so doing restore it as the international monetary standard.

But even in struggling to enact these measures, we should not allow ourselves to believe that our objective is aggregate economic output, or to think of the American economy as a table of statistics: widgets produced, hours worked, employment percentages. We want to excite the elusive but vital qualities of human ingenuity and effort, qualities important not only to an economy increasingly dominated by sophisticated services, but to the well-being and happiness of our nation's people. Ingenuity is discovered only through effort, an intangible substance which certainly means more, much more, than putting in hours. After all, some people manage to retire on the job. Effort encompasses such things as a continual eagerness to acquire new knowledge and skills, a willingness to accept new responsibilities, to take the risks of initiating change. Effort can only be measured indirectly, by results, and the results are not only measured by personal prosperity but by the enrichment of community life as well.

This is still a nation of people who are able and anxious to fix things, to solve problems in ways the slothful never dream of. We have 37 million people in this country doing volunteer work to better their communities and to assist their neighbors. We have thousands of block associations in New York City providing the very best kind of security —mutual concern. We are seeing revitalization of some older urban neighborhoods in places like Baltimore, Philadelphia, and Buffalo—with a minimum of government direction. The American dream is not one of getting ahead at the expense of our neighbors—not of dividing and redistributing. It is the dream of general progress arising from individual creativity and initiative—the dream of a rising tide.

To me, this kind of renewal can be the only force behind an American renaissance. For what I envision as the objective of governmental reforms and tax strategies goes beyond the material to the spiritual. The creative genius that has always invigorated America is still there, submerged, waiting like a genie in a bottle to be loosed. It is not something that can be quantified by a government economist or statistician, but we know it when we feel it. The ultimate goal is not to add another $100 billion to gross national product by adding so many widget factories and so many smokestacks. The history of America's creative energy has indeed resulted in the production of more, but it has also resulted in the production of better; and when we are on course, all of us as individuals should feel we are in some way improving the human condition. Only during this recent shadowy period of our history have we witnessed the decline of quality and the elevation of quantity, the result of our waning confidence in ourselves as a nation. This, though, is what one would expect when the system itself blocks the individual fulfillment of individual potential. An American renaissance must be a renaissance of the American spirit that can only come when that spirit can soar.

We are still left with the capacity to turn nuts on assembly lines, but our ability to call up creativity and resourcefulness steadily declines, to the point where as a nation we produce little that is memorable (perhaps because this is not a period we might wish to remember). Quality, Golden Ages—in architecture, sports, arts and letters, music and motion pictures, and yes, ethics—cannot be punched out by a bored work force begrudgingly doing its chores. Such periods of quality are possible only when everyone has the opportunity to reach as high as he can, relentlessly pushing against the boundless frontiers of intelligence and creativity.

In his *Harper's* article, George Gilder had this thought:

> To many people, the past seems inevitable and the future impossible. History is seen to have arisen not from unpredictable flows of genius and heroism, but more or less inevitably, from preordained patterns of natural resources and population. For those who doubt the decisive

role of genius, courage, and chance in history, the future always appears impossible; they can see no way for free nations to escape a fate of decline, decay, and coercion, as their growing populations press against a closing frontier.

The truth is, no frontier need be closed for long. Yes, the rich, bountiful earth is limited in what it can provide, but there are no natural bounds to the human spirit and its accomplishments, except insofar as we are cramped by human timidity and fear or by human institutions. In the 1980s, the first decade of the American renaissance, these are the bounds we must pit ourselves against, so it can be said of our nation in our time, "To her, and to her especially, belongs the future."

Index